THE

SKEPTICAL ERA

IN MODERN HISTORY;

OR,

The Infidelity of the Eighteenth Century,

THE PRODUCT OF SPIRITUAL DESPOTISM.

BY T. M. POST.

NEW YORK:
CHARLES SCRIBNER, 145 NASSAU STREET.

1856.

W. H. TINSON, STEREOTYPER. GEORGE RUSSELL & CO., PRINTERS.

PREFACE.

FREEDOM and Faith are the great Tutelar Forces of modern civilization. Their relation to each other is the great problem of the age; one whose solution has with it the destiny of the future. The question presses on us with the more solemn aspect, the more evident becomes the hastening approach of an era of democratic liberty in church, state, and society. What condition of the religious sentiment will consort with that political and social order of the world? Will faith consist with it? If so, will it be a vigorous, vital, commanding, organic element, or is it destined to be timid and feeble, holding with unbelief a doubtful and divided empire?

A philosophic writer, eminent for accurate and profound social analysis, De Tocqueville, thus gives his solution of the above problem. "I am inclined to believe that our posterity in the democratic ages will tend more and more to a single division into two parts; some relinquishing Christianity entirely, others returning to the bosom of the Church of Rome." That is, in the ages of democratic freedom, spiritual despotism will be the only conservator of faith.

Chateaubriand also, in his "Études Historiques" claims

for Catholicism that it is the religion of democratic society, whilst he characterizes the Reformed Faith as "*Philosophic truth, clothed with Christian form, attacking religious truth*"—having achieved for society a change from the military to the civil and industrial genius, and "able to point, amid the ruins it has wrought, simply to *some field it has planted*, and *some manufactures it has established*." Nor are these writers alone in their forecast of the future, or their estimate of the relations of Protestantism to democracy and faith. Sentiments like the above are rife in the literature of the day. They are the cant of a school; a school not of the Catholic communion alone. Protestant writers of profound and tasteful culture, of devout and earnest tone, and of a seductive plausibility and grace, join in their utterance.

Protestantism, they tell you, is a religion of negations; its philosophy that of doubt, denial, irreverence and insurrection; its triumphs logical, economic, administrative, industrial, fiscal; its genius cold, hard, practical, materialistic; unheroic, unideal, undevout—the very antipodes of exalted religious passion or faith. These are to find shelter alone under the shadow of an ecclesiastical absolutism. Thus the democratic ages are to be the millennium of spiritual despotism; both because such despotism will, by natural affinity attract those ages, and because it alone will be able to keep alive religious sentiment and belief during their progress. Thus, in many quarters Protestantism seems afraid of its own life-principles, and verging towards the suicide of renouncing them. But before joining in this deadly work, we are compelled to pause and inquire. Is the above solution of the religious problem of society the true one? Is despotism the only keeper of faith? An era of entire liberty, of necessity, an era of unbelief? What facts authorize an augury so gloomy? The advocates of sentiments above alluded to, claim that history makes for them, and point in proof to the infidel cycle following the Lutheran reform. The era of irreligious eclipse and the catastrophe of the world which closed it, they arraign as crimes of liberty—of Protestantism. It was this, they argue, which poisoned modern civilization. It was this which, by the revolution in philosophy, and the insurrection of mind against authority, which it inaugurated; and by the dethronement of the religious idea and the enthronement of that of wealth over European civilization, wrought the ruin of the world's faith. This was to society the fountain of doubt and irreverence, and of materialism, sensualism, and Mammonism, that corrupted the world and prepared its overthrow.

But it has seemed to the writer of this work, that their very witness confutes them; that it requires no very acute or profound analysis to trace the infidelity of the eighteenth century to a widely different source. To ascribe the skepticism of the eighteenth century to the religious revolution of the sixteenth, is to ascribe a stream to the cascade down which its waters may have previously flowed. It were as philosophical to attribute to the overflow of a dammed-up flood gushing down one side its reservoir, its resurgent overflow on another. Such a cascade, was the Lutheran reform, in the progress of modern mind: such a flow and resurgent overflow from the dammed-up flood of European thought, were the religious and philosophical revolutions of the sixteenth and eighteenth centuries—independent consequences of a common force.

Another cause, patent and portentous, stands out in Ætnean prominence in that landscape of ruin—a cause, the direct antithesis of liberty. To trace this cause, to show its wide-spread mischievousness, imparting a malign efficiency to causes merely secondary or occasional, and to exhibit its essential and implacable hostility to genuine faith, is the aim of these pages ; an aim pursued through the relations, historical and philosophical, of the phenomenon we are considering.

In pursuance of this aim, I have first attempted to *exhibit the fact* we are to explain—the nature and extent of that strange defection of faith that marked the eighteenth century. We, then, consider its causes ; and first those which are secondary and occasional ; such as *e. g.*, the low and relaxed moral tone of the world's mind at the time the epidemic of unbelief set in—the century and a half of religious agonism and arms which preceded the revolution in philosophy inaugurated by Bacon and Des Cartes in physics and metaphysics, and by Luther in the realm of religion—and the rise of the idea of wealth to the ascendency in cabinets of governments, and in general society. Our view is then directed to the "*Fons et origo malorum*," the great CAUSE OF CAUSES of the evil we investigate ; viz : despotism, despotism both secular and spiritual, but with especial and portentous preëminence of the latter. Our investigation then, brings us to the geographic focus and centre of the plague :—France. Its position in European civilization—its civil and ecclesiastical constitution and history—its court, monarchy, church, literature—these are seen through the malign influence of spiritual despotism, directed to the subversion of belief ; and finally resulting in the organization of a conspiracy and crusade against the faith of the world.

Having traced the evil cause above noted, *i. e.*, despotism, to its consequences in France, we next inquire into its effects in other countries of Europe,—those especially claimed by spiritual despotism as monuments of her power to guard nations from infidelity—viz.: Italy and Spain. A brief view of the manner in which she has conserved faith in the two peninsulas closes our survey.

Such is in general the plan and aim of this work. If I shall have been to any degree thereby instrumental of adding in any mind to the elements of hopefulness and courage in the solution of the great problem indicated, or of giving confidence to the confession of the great principles of Protestant liberty, or shall have contributed aught to vindicate for the human soul prerogatives claimed by its imperishable instincts, warranted by the great charter of its faith, I shall feel that this humble effort is not altogether without service to the Great King of truth to whom it is my wish to dedicate it.

T. M. P.

St. Louis, Oct. 20, 1855.

CONTENTS.

CHAPTER I.

THE SKEPTICISM OF THE EIGHTEENTH CENTURY, ITS CHARACTER AND EXTENT.

The Skeptical Era in Modern History—An Eclipse—The Arsenal of conflicting Philosophic Schools—Skepticism, the Epidemic of the world through an entire Historic Cycle—Its changing Genius—Skepticism in Literature—In Philosophy—The Philosophic Anarchs and Revolutionists—Skepticism in Belles-lettres, Criticism, Art, Poetry, History, Oratory—Skepticism in Place and Power—Frederick of Prussia, Joseph of Austria, and Catherine of Russia—Skepticism in the Million—Skepticism becomes a Fanaticism—A Nemesis—The Infidelity of the Eighteenth Century; more a War with Facts than Creeds; more with the Church than Christianity—Its geographic Origin and Theatre 9

CHAPTER II.

CAUSE OF THE INFIDELITY OF THE EIGHTEENTH CENTURY.

A century and a half precedent of Religious Passion and War; Relaxation, Exhaustion, and Reaction consequent—Position of the Religious Liberties of Nations at its close—Dethronement of the Religious Idea—Causes and Consequences—Religious Wars—Who was responsible for them and their Mischiefs to Faith—Aspect of the World at the opening of the Skeptical Era melancholy and portentous—Its Lessons 36

CHAPTER III.

REVOLUTION IN PHILOSOPHY.

Revolution in Philosophy—A necessity of Social Progress perverted by Spiritual Despotism to the destruction of Faith—Protestantism a Revolutionist in Philosophy—Different Philosophic Methods—Aristotelian—Scholastic—Baconian—Mediæval Philosophy, the instrument of Spiritual Despotism—Aristotle and the Pope, Joint Monarchs and High Priests of Thought and Faith—Revolution in Philosophy, an emancipation of mind—Its position in the Map of Modern History—Eras of Religious, Philosophical, and Political Revolution—Futility and fruitlessness of the Old Philosophy—A barren toil in an endless circle—A blind and fetter of Mind—Its Overthrow a Necessity—Why it dragged Faith with it in its Fall—Different Results in different Countries—Disasters to Faith, the result of Spiritual Despotism—Protestantism as Revolutionist in Philosophy a mighty Benefactor—Plea of the Baconian Philosophy 57

CHAPTER IV.

MAMMONISM.

Rise of the Idea of Wealth to the Ascendency in European Society—Causes—Subsidence of Religious Passions—Old paths of National Aggrandizement closed up—Transfer of Ambition and Enterprise to new Desertions—Progress of Society in Wealth and Productive Art—The Era of Economies—Mississippi Schemes—East Indies—Ventures—South Sea Bubbles—The Money-God Supreme—The new Philosophy his Minister—Acme of his Reign at Paris under the Regent of Orleans—Law's Banking Scheme—The Saturnalia of Mammon—Rise of the Idea of Wealth a Necessity of Social Progress—Why so Disastrous to Faith?—Money-mania in France and England Compared—Dangers to Modern Society from Mammonism 91

CHAPTER V.

SPIRITUAL DESPOTISM.

Spiritual Despotism, the Cause of Causes—Era of Absolutism—Double Despotism over Europe—Treaty of Westphalia—Military

Monarchies—Hopelessness and helplessness of the Millions—Intellectual repression—Mind driven from the Practical to the Speculative—License of Speculative Thought—The World Undermined—War on Private Judgment—A War on the Faith of Nations—The Spiritual Power Darkened and Emasculated—Intellectual imbecility of the Church—Ecclesiastical Literature in Protestant and Catholic Europe 117

CHAPTER VI.

SPIRITUAL DESPOTISM.

Despotism Corrupts the Spiritual Power, through Hierarchy, Confessional, Celibacy, Separation of Power from the People ; Peculiar Corruptions of Politico-Ecclesiastical Despotism, especially around the Thrones of Central Europe, in the 17th and 18th centuries—Cardinal Dubois—Regent of Orleans—Louis 15th—Christianity made a Religion of Force—Terrible pressure of Spiritual Despotism in the precedent ages—Reaction as the Force applied—England and France compared—Christianity hated of the Nations as the ally of Secular Tyranny—Infidelity from Superstition—from Infallibility—Essential and immortal malignancy of Spiritual Despotism 144

CHAPTER VII.

FRANCE.

France the most Powerful Generator and Diffuser of Infidelity—Her Position in Modern History—The Model Kingdom of Europe—Oracle of Civilization—Her Early Culture—Genius—Language—Court Literature—Political Ascendency—Self-diffusiveness—Causes of Infidelity in her Civil and Ecclesiastic Constitution and History—Religious Wars—Albigenses—Huguenots—Separation of the Actual from the Ideal the widest—Reaction of Repressed Mind most Passionate—Daring and Revolutionary Despotism in France in the 17th and 18th Centuries—Absolutism of Louis XIV.—Its Mischief—Two Great Crimes of the French Church and Monarchy Generative of Infidelity — Ecclesiastic Barbarism extending down toward the close of the 18th Century—Torture and Execution at Abbeville 1776—Despotism in France applied to a Mind the most Active, Daring, Witty and Philosophic in Europe 177

CHAPTER VIII.

FRANCE.

French Literature of the 18th century—Infidel Writers and Savans—Mission of Infidelity organized—Its Apostles and Evangelists, Voltaire, Rousseau, and the Encyclopedists—Their Quarry, the French church—Its Corruption, Ignorance, Superstitions and Cruelties—Jesuitism—Its Exposé and Fall—Money-madness in France—The Primal Fountain of her Infidelity—Politico-Ecclesiastical Despotism 203

CHAPTER IX.

SPIRITUAL DESPOTISM IN ITALY AND SPAIN.

ITALY—Spiritual Despotism a generator of Infidelity in Italy and Spain—Italian History mutilated and stifled—Its silence significant—Insurrection of Mind indicated by the measures of Repression—Their Multitude and Atrocity—Censorships—Proscriptions—Crusades—Massacres—Dominicans—Franciscans—The Inquisition—Glimpses of Infidelity in Italian History and Literature—Infidelity a necessity of Pontifical History applied to the Italian mind—The Troubadour—Dante—Petrarch—Arnold of Brescia—Savonarola—Infidel Scholars—Monarchs—Popes—Repressive measures of the Sixteenth Century—Their utter mercilessness—Terror—Silence—Italy stifled but not believing 229

SPAIN.—Orthodoxy of Spain—No Spasm in a Corpse—The Inquisition, the instrument of Spanish Faith—Its mystery and terror—War on Books—Index Expurgatorus—Death struggle of the Spanish mind, 1559-1570—Spanish Thought, Literature, Civilization, Manhood fall together—Silence not belief—The Peninsula still seething with insurgent Infidelity—Three Realms of Spiritual Despotism compared 246

CONCLUSION.

Résumé of the Argument—Lessons for the Times—Doom of Spiritual Despotism 256

CHAPTER I.

THE SKEPTICISM OF THE EIGHTEENTH CENTURY.

ITS CHARACTER AND EXTENT.

The Skeptical Era in Modern History---An Eclipse—The Arsenal of conflicting Philosophic Schools—Skepticism, the Epidemic of the world through an entire Historic Cycle—Its changing Genius—Skepticism in Literature—In Philosophy—The Philosophic Anarchs and Revolutionists—Skepticism in Belles-lettres, Criticism, Art, Poetry, History, Oratory—Skepticism in Place and Power—Frederick of Prussia, Joseph of Austria, and Catherine of Russia—Skepticism in the Million—Skepticism becomes a Fanaticism—A Nemesis—The Infidelity of the Eighteenth Century; more a War with Facts than Creeds; more with the Church than Christianity—Its geographic Origin and Theatre.

THE period through which our proposed discussion conducts us, was eminently the skeptical era in modern history; an era brilliant, powerful, daring, but melancholy and ruinous. It bequeathed to the Present, lessons of vast import. The eighteenth century may be fitly defined a period of Religious Eclipse in modern civilization. The definition is significant and descriptive of the fact.

The period was one of deep and wide occultation of the religious element in modern civilization—an eclipse, not a sunset—for the orb of Christian Light and Life was still climbing the skies. The world passed into profound shade—but though dark and chill, it was not the shadow of night. It was an eclipse in which the satellite lunar orb—the reflector of the great central light—came between the earth and that light. The CHURCH intervened between God and the world, between humanity and Jesus Christ, and history consequently moves on through a cycle of lurid and disastrous gloom.

It is a period of profound interest in the study of the Past. The Infidelity of the eighteenth century is as important a theme as the revolution which sprang from it. It is a period of startling contrasts; according to aspects presented from different points of view, it is the most hopeful or most fearful, the most disastrous or most successful, the most glorious or most shameful in modern history; and it throws its light and gloom over the age in which we are, and down the distant future. These very contrasts and the multiformity of aspects make it one of solemn and varied significance, and of profoundest instruction. They have made it also the "*locus communis*"—the commonplace topic—of argument or warning, of vindication or invective, for opposite schools of ecclesiastical and social philosophers; the arsenal from which the absolutist and the liberal, the conservative and the reformer, the reactionary and the progressive, the Romanist and the Protestant, alike derive their weapons; each challenging it as argument and justification of itself and as the condemnation and scandal of its antagonist.

The one school regards this era as almost sheerly infernal; the other views it as bringing with its crime and ruin, vast blessings; but both alike brandish, each at the other, its sins and its shames, in derision and anathema, as the direct and necessary sequence of its adversary's distinctive principles. But read the phenomena of the proposed period differently as they may, all parties unite in regarding it as furnishing lessons of vast import for society and the church in our age.

We purpose as we may be able to read and interpret these lessons; to inquire *what causes* pushed society for such a period upon such a career of illusion, impiety, and ruin. We may have occasion to track to their historic consequences, principles of antagonistic philosophical and ecclesiastic schools that are contending for the possession of our age; and may be able thus in looking over this page of history, blotted so much with tears and blood and shame, to detect dangers that attach to the present, and catch glimpses of a prophecy projected down the future. A chapter that has cost so much and effected so much for humanity, ought not to pass without imparting important instructions. As the readiest means of deriving those instructions, we propose to investigate and track to historic origin, the great central fact of the period—the germ and exponent of its moral disease—its SKEPTICISM, and to interrogate it both as cause and effect.

Whence then arose that occultation of faith that darkened Europe during the last part of the seventeenth, and the entire course of the eighteenth century? striking through society with chill and paralysis during the first part of this period, emasculating and corrupting it, and finally draping its sunset in crimson glooms?

But first, let us endeavor to describe and define the phenomenon we propose to investigate. Let us aim rightly to conceive of that strange and portentous condition of the world's mind, we are to analyze, and trace to its origin.

The phenomenon is as patent as it is baleful; is one fearfully unique, one most distinctively marked. It stands in the landscape of the past, in the prominence of a volcanic mountain, strange, unmistakable, portentous. It is the great feature of a historic cycle. It strikes one at the first glance that some strangely malignant and disastrous influences must have moved on the human mind during the eighteenth century, to drive it from the regions of faith.

Infidelity is undoubtedly ever more or less prevalent in society. The ultimate philosophy of this is unquestionally that announced by the Apostle: "men do not choose to retain God in their knowledge." Man hid from his God in Eden, and his history is full of the same attempt: so it will be to the end. "When the son of man cometh, shall He find faith on the earth?" is our Saviour's significant inquiry.

But in the historic view before us, it is the *epidemic of the world for a century.* A moral plague has struck through Christendom—through its entire thought and feeling, its manners, literature, legislation, its philosophy, its poetry, its oratory; through all its private and public life; through all its social order from the camp to the altar, and from the galley to the throne; and through its domestic and international politics. It imbues the European mind and life as a master feeling; yea at last, strange as it may seem for a thing ordinarily so feeble as unbelief, as a master passion: all Europe hisses with a scoffing skepticism which gradually changes to a scream of maniac rage. The genius of unbelief presides everywhere. In the chamber of the voluptuary, the academy of the savant, the conclave of hierarchies, the salons of the witty and beautiful, and finally in national assemblies tempestuous with revolution, it sits—not a Miltonic Satan "with the starry grandeur of darkness" on his brow, defiant though believing and despairing—but a sneering Mephistophiles, in whose glance the flowers of Christian civilization wither. Honor, honesty, chastity as well as piety, seem to flee like Astrea of old from the earth. Fraud, cunning, perfidy, avarice, creep like a chill malaria through all the highways and by-ways of the world. With them accompany sensualism, luxury, prodigality, and cruel rapacity. Between nations public law is prostrated; faith and morality seem perished. The great European family of states seems converted into a band of picaroons and robbers, now uniting, now quarrelling on the question of mutual dismemberment and plunder. First Saxony, then Maria Theresa of Austria, then Frederick of Prussia, and finally, unhappy Poland, present the quarry for these conspiracies of miscreant cabinets.

Everywhere men doubt, disbelieve, deny; and in regard to every interest. Under the deadly paralysis, the society of the world seems going into dissolution; all its ordinary bands are unloosed. There is no God in its temples; no sincerity in its worship; no belief in its creed; no morality in its policy or practice. The soul of the world seems materialized, sensualized, mammonized. Society is dying of the want of faith—faith in religion or in virtue—faith in man or in God. With faith perishing have perished heroism and truth, chivalry and law; and the order of the world is undermined. At first the malady of which we speak, strikes through Christendom as a cold plague; but toward the close of the period we are reviewing, it changes to a delirious fever. The Mephistophiles of the first act, appears at the catastrophe an avenging flaming Apollyon.

If in proof and illustration of the above statements we look at some of the various departments of thought and action in those ages, at some of the great thinkers and actors in them, we find writers of every class; legists, publicists, statesmen, poets, philosophers, economists, ecclesiastics; we find also courts, kings, generals, hierarchs and the general spirit and tendencies of the masses, all imbued with a religious skepticism.

First let us look at the utterance of the era in its literature. This we find almost universally skeptical. We shudder at its bad eminence in this respect, at the human mind for a century of most mighty, successful and brilliant achievement, constantly expending its energies against the Most High; lifting like a mad Titan against the pillars of elder civilization—against its faith, philosophy and order; and in its struggle to emancipate itself, hurling its broken fetters at the throne of God. We tremble when we contemplate the dark inundation of corrupting thought poured forth like a river of infernal night for one hundred years on the mind of the world! and, how the floods of an ungodly literature gather around the city of our God! reason, philosophy, eloquence, imagination, leading on the attack: poesy, art, wit, grace and beauty hanging their glittering banners above the impious onset. Truly, "The floods have lifted up, O Lord, the floods have lifted up their voice. The floods lifted up their waves. But the Lord on high was mightier than many waters, yea, than the mighty waves of the sea."

Guizot characterized the eighteenth century as one distinguished from its predecessors by the fact, that in it the *human mind* seems the supreme and almost sole actor, to the comparative exclusion of cabinets and governments. It was one also in which the human mind appears animated by a spirit of universal free inquiry, making everything the subject of question, doubt and system; avenging itself for its exclusion from affairs, by the most daring and boundless license in the realms of speculative thought; and in that realm respecting no external fact or institution, and standing in awe before no authority and no principle. Such a mind looks forth on you from all its literature. You admire its freedom and power; are appalled at its irreverence and impiety. You tremble when you think of the shock that must ensue when the ideal world it builds, shall come, as it must in time, in collision with the Actual.

Such is the general spirit of all thought during this period. That in the domain of literature, it should have taken primary and especial possession of *philosophy*, was natural. Here obviously it must have entrenched itself. Here we know, must have been its citadel, if not its fountain. But we are startled to note the *extent* to which it seems to be held, as by demoniacal possession, with a spirit of universal Skepticism, and armed only with the logic of insurrection and destruction. The foundations of *all* belief are sapped by it. It boldly questions everything. It revolutionizes the primal method and the first principles of all faith. It applies its skeptical method to all departments and to every interest; finance, political economy, chemistry, natural history—to physics and mathematics as well as to logic, ethics and criticism; and in these it works much beneficient emancipation and reform. It applies its revolutionary method to questions of social order—to politics, laws, the institutions of public and private life, to manners, marriage, property, government, and finally to religion. All these it undermines; the order of the world topples over an abyss. From Montaigne, Montesquieu, Voltaire and Rousseau, to the last of the Gironde, the leading minds of France—the centre and model of European civilization—had labored in this work of undermining with the might and brilliancy of fallen spirits. "From the seat of geometry to the consecrated pulpit," says Lamartine, "the philosophy of the eighteenth century had invaded and altered everything. D'Alembert, Diderot, Condorcet, Bernardin de Saint Pierre, Helvetius, La Harpe were the church of the new era. One sole thought animated these minds—the revolution of ideas. Arithmetic, science, history, society, economy, politics, the stage, morals, poetry—all seemed as a vehicle of the modern philosophy. It ran through all the veins of the times. It had enlisted every genius, spoke every language."

From Louis XIV. to Louis XVI. the age had been prodigal of great men in France. All these an infidel philosophy had drawn within its train, and formed of them a constellation of such brilliancy, that it drew the gaze and worship of mankind—made Paris the Rome or Babylon of European civilization.

Amid these philosophic anarchs and revolutionists, Voltaire, Rousseau, Diderot and their compeers, badly eminent as they were, belong to the moderates compared with the schools that sprang from them.

Wide and fearful was the abyss they opened; but beneath that depth "a lower deep" still yawned—a deep below the throne of God, below the very religion of nature. In this, with infernal daring and hate, labored the cohort of the atheist philosophers and anarchs of the revolution, aiming to whelm in one ruin not only Christianity and Deism, but all moral distinctions and ideas. Virtue, vice, right, wrong, with moral government, law, retribution, marriage, property—all were figments of superstition, long mocking and vexing man; the banishment of which, together with the vanishing humbugs of God, Immortality, Heaven and Hell, was to inaugurate the Golden Age. To this foul crew belonged the obscene and bloody fanatics of unbelief that formed the pageant of the Goddess of Reason of 1792.

The doctrines of this school are identified by Menzel, in his History of Literature, with those of Heine, who, though of a subsequent generation, may be regarded as representative and disciple of the same school. His impious ravings are only the echo of the "Free Philosophy," so called, and for convenience sake, may here be given as a résumé of it:

"Heine," says Menzel, "called Christianity a miserable and bloody religion for criminals, and Christ a haggard, bloody Jew, who had robbed the world of all its joys, and destroyed the beautiful religion of Paganism." "He paints before us how the whole garrison of Heaven must be put to the sword. How God is weltering in his blood, and immortality is lying at its last gasp. He declares the distinction between good and evil only a crazy dream of Christianity; that there is no such thing as vice; that nature is divine; that nature may allow itself in every indulgence and never sin. Matter is God. Sensual enjoyment alone is holy. Sensual festivals must take the place of Christian ordinances. After submitting to oppression so long, the senses must avenge themselves by orgies of uninterrupted debauchery. All mankind must constitute themselves into a republic of the happy, and no longer toil and starve, but eat pies, drink sack, and embrace fair flesh."

But enough; the above may suffice to show the deeps to which the sensational philosophy had sunk, and was aiming to drag down society.

Thus everywhere had the disciples of the new philosphy labored in their bad vocation, till they had unsettled the faith of Christendom, and brought society to the verge of an abyss. Thought everywhere was skeptical and revolutionary—the human mind everywhere insurgent against the traditionary, the old, the revered; and everywhere moving on over the wrecks of philosophic systems and religious faith, to the destruction of all the outward forms and the vital order of society; a deadly gilded illusion beckoning it onward, and projecting a golden age on what proved, as the illusion faded, a dark, weltering, bloody chaos.

Nor was this skeptical tendency restricted to any peculiar philosophic school. The sensational, the ideal, the mystic—the disciples of Des Cartes and Kant, as well as of Locke, on the continent at least, develop this disastrous bias; with all degrees of doubting indeed, but all moving the same darkening way to absolute unbelief. So much did this melancholy tendency mark the age, that those who were themselves devout and earnest believers, seemed, through the use or abuse of the philosophic systems which they originated or advocated, transmuted by the all-pervading spirit of the age into abettors of unbelief and irreligion. Thus Locke, Des Cartes, Malebranche, Leibnitz, and even Fénélon and Pascal by the consequences to which their principles were driven, seemed forced into strange coadjutorship with Diderot, Helvetius, and Voltaire. Hobbes, Gassendi, Kant, and Spinoza, are succeeded by those who, from the want of harmonizing and limiting eclecticism, taking up their principles, carried them to wild extravagances of skepticism and misbelief, and not unfrequently to atrocious dissoluteness and stark atheism.

Helvetius, Holbach, Hébert, Chaumette, Cloots, Marat follow on. Finally, all ends in a bloody debauch of blasphemous anarchy. As in time of pestilence all diseases run into the prevailing disease or assume its type, so in the eighteenth century all moral and intellectual distemperatures, running directly to religious skepticism, make it as the *epidemic* malady of the era. In England the sensational philosophy speedily becomes skeptical, as in case of Hobbes and Hume. In France the philosophy of Locke transplanted had brought forth the fruit of a gross materialism which warred on God, the soul, and immortality—a mere creed of insurrection and destruction directed against the social, political, and religious world. Voltaire and Rousseau were the great apostles of this gospel of unbelief; the encyclopædists, expounders, and evangelists; and from Paris, the philosophic Jerusalem, it had gone forth to possess the nations,

> "As from the Python's mystic cave of yore,
> The oracles that set the world in flame,
> Nor ceased to burn till kingdoms were no more."

"The whole history of the literary society of France during the latter half of the eighteenth century," says Morell, "is but a comment on the progress of sensationalism towards its ultimate climax. The school of Voltaire shows the effect of it while still incomplete and shrinking from the hard materialism, that blind fatality and daring atheism, to which it afterward attained. But the encyclopædia is its great embodiment. Man is to it but a mass of organization; mind the development of our sensations; morality is self-interest, and God the diseased fiction of an unenlightened and enthusiastic age."

In other countries of central Europe the idealism of Des Cartes had passed through Spinoza to Pantheism, or had hardened to adamantine mechanic fatalism; or as in Germany, pushing all belief into the region of myths and dreams, it had overcast the whole land with doubts and phantasms, till it seemed as though the ivory gate through which, according to ancient fables, wicked illusions and lying phantoms went forth from the underworld to abuse mankind, had opened from underneath it, and had sent forth glittering inanities to wander over Europe. The process through which the sensational and ideal systems alike led to infidelity, is not relevant to my aim to note. I mark simply as indicating the tendency of the age, the fact that both alike conducted to unbelief.

Thus had PHILOSOPHY labored in the eighteenth century in the destruction of Faith. She brought to humanity vast blessings. She emancipated the human mind; but in tearing down the walls of its prison, she tore down also temple and throne. Her sons, a mighty brood—mighty for good or ill—stand before us in the landscape of that age, like the sons of Elder Night on the lightning-blasted plains of Phlegra.

"Their steep aim was Titan-like, on daring doubts to pile,
Thoughts which should call down thunder.
They made themselves a fearful monument,
The wreck of old opinion, things which grew
Breathed from the birth of time. The veil they rent,
And what behind it lay, all Earth shall view.
But good with ill, they also overthrew,
Leaving but ruins."

If we look at other departments of literature, we find the same distemperature of skepticism circulating in the veins of all of them. Through all *Belles-lettres* and *fiction* it insinuated itself; from the romance of Marmontel, St. Pierre and the Heloise of

"The self-torturing sophist—wild Rousseau, who knew
How to make madness beautiful, and cast
O'er erring deeds and thoughts a heavenly hue,
Of words like sunbeams, dazzling as they passed;"—

from these to the nameless and abominable herd of

miscreant novelists that drugged and intoxicated the French mind before and in the saturnalia of the Revolution, it pervaded all.

Criticism was possessed by the same genius of unbelief. This glittered in its wit: this hissed in its sneer. Dipped in its venom flew thick and fast the dreaded shafts from Ferney over Europe, striking down the titled, the gifted, and the mighty, smiting alike monarch and mistress, scholar and soldier, poet and priest.

Art was minister to unbelief. Its ideas were bodied in the marble and glowed on the canvas or breathed in music.

Poetry sang of it. It insinuated itself through the charm of imagination and measure, from the epic march of the Henriade and the epigrammatic sneer of the drama, to the ballad-monger of the Revolution.

History was its vehicle. Through numerous writers on the continent, as well as Hume and Gibbon in England, "sapping a solemn creed with a solemn sneer," it held the colored glass of infidelity between the eye of Europe and the most interesting personages and periods in human story.

Eloquence was infidel; as in the Æolus-cave of National Convention, it stormed against monarchs, hierarchs, human tyrannies and even the throne of the Highest, challenging and arraigning all; impleading at the bar of a wrathful age, all the abuses of the past, the crimes of a lying faith, and of a despotic Church and State, and alas, with these, Christianity and Civilization itself, for sentence and execution.

Thus the pestilence of infidelity had struck through the world's universal thought. It flowed in the lucid charm of Montaigne, it pointed an envenomed article in the Dictionary of Philosophy, it breathed its spirit into Montesquieu's Spirit of the Laws, it struck its coloring through Universal Science in the Encyclopædia. It sparkled in epigrammatic impieties in the theatres of Paris, Vienna and Petersburg; it looked forth from the picture galleries of Versailles and Potsdam. It breathed through the seductive profanities of Helvetius, it glittered in the beautiful sophisms of the Social Contract and in the tears of the Letters from the Mountains. It spread its charm through the Theophilanthropic dreams of Marmontel or the sensual pictures of Le Clos. It travelled and meditated with Volney 'mid ancient ruins; it shed its false light over Gibbon's magnificent pageant of a past world, from the moonlight solitudes of the mouldering Coliseum.

Nor did the skepticism of the eighteenth century confine itself to writers and thinkers. Power, place, the mode had become infidel; monarch and courtier, statesman and general, priest and prelate sported their infidelity in the salons of Paris, Berlin, Vienna and Petersburg. Catharine of Russia, Joseph of Austria, Frederick of Prussia, as well as the most powerful and brilliant figures of the French Court, were enthusiastic disciples and propagandists of the new philosophy. Frederick and Catharine were constant and admiring correspondents of Voltaire, D'Alembert and Diderot, and were wont to close their letters with the sobriquet "crush the wretch" applied to Christianity, and especially to the French Church. Frederick furnished Voltaire an ample establishment at Berlin, and was ever ambitious of having a coterie of infidel literati around him. Indeed Frederick and Voltaire may be taken as representative types of the era in its crimes, its meanness and impiety, as well as in its order of heroism and genius. Catharine in her last days saw her error—or at least its aspect of attack on despotic order in Europe—and grieved lest in consequence of her encouragement of French philosophy, she might be arraigned in history as the cause of the Revolution. Graver crimes, which overlaid this with crimson, might have relieved her of her fears. Still, to some extent undoubtedly, she with her fellow despots of that age, would have to plead guilty even to that charge.

But it is instructive and worthy of remark how little aware were the potentates of that period of what they were doing; how unconsciously they admired, caressed and fawned on their deadliest foe. They played and toyed with the tiger-kitten, and admired its sleek grace and velvety paw, and feline caprices, till at once it stood before them a full-grown monster whose scream for blood sent shuddering and paleness through the Palace of Royalty and the Chamber of Pleasure.

Nor had infidelity meanwhile simply taken possession of the high places of Literature and Courts. From the learned and the noble it had spread through the *masses*. It had taken from the oppressed millions, their chief solace for suffering and their chief aid to virtue, their belief in God and immortality. Henceforth they had no friend above, no judge, no vindicator on high. This life of woes and shams and shames was their all. It is no wonder they turned in the madness of revenge and of desperate pleasure-seeking, on their oppressors and all old order. An awful responsibility rests somewhere for the frightful wrongs wrought to the millions of that era, in the destruction of their religious faith; and terrible was the hour of retribution which could not fail to come.

How frightfully diffused was not only a disbelief

of religion, but a savage hate, a rage even against Christianity, the insurrections of nations at the time of the French Revolution not only against monarchy, but Christianity, wreaking their fanatical atrocities not only against the Church, but against all that was called God, furnish terrible proofs. This indeed forms one of the most melancholy and fearful of the features of the infidelity of that period—the fact, that unbelief became a *fanaticism, a passion of hatred and fury against Christianity.* It is a feature full of significance, one demanding investigation, and which will throw light upon the question of the cause of the infidelity of the age. We are arrested by this feature. We pause over it in wonder and sorrow. Why that sentiment of the stricken, blind, haggard millions—that sentiment of unbelief changing to a flaming rage against the great champion of the poor and the oppressed—Jesus Christ? What must have been the aspect of that Christ exhibited by that body that professed to be his representative among men—the church—to draw upon such a character the storming phrenzy of nations? This is a question we have to consider, and we shall be led to inquire in whose skirts is the blood of this mighty guilt. What hand was it that held up a travestied, deformed Christ before the millions? Among the millions of what nominal communion, under what ecclesiastic banner, in the domain of what church, did this strange madness break out? But of this, more hereafter. It suffices our present aim of sketching with general feature and coloring the phenomenon we investigate, to note that for some cause, as we near the close of the eighteenth century, this melancholy and malignant aspect of unbelief strikes us portentously everywhere. Doubt has become wrath. The cold plague has changed to phrenzy and fever. Unbelief has itself become a religion, armed with fanaticism and rage. As we look out on the nations of central Europe the view seems frightful. There is a strange agitation of peoples insurgent against Heaven; a tumultuous "noise of the kingdoms of nations mustering to the battle against the Most High and His anointed." In the perspective of that age, we seem looking out on a landscape stretching under the cope of eternal night; where the armies of evil are battling against a sky dark and thunderous with wrath. We have before us Milton's terrible picture of the impious rage of the fallen millions of eternal night and woe—that revel of infinite rage and infinite despair, wherein

> "Outflew
> "Millions of flaming swords, drawn from the thighs
> Of mighty cherubim: the sudden blaze
> Far round illumined Hell; highly they raged

Against the highest, and fierce with grasped arms,
Clashed on their sounding shields the din of war,
Hurling defiance at the vault of Heaven."

The catastrophe of European states and society well-nigh subverting modern civilization itself, that closes the eighteenth century, does not surprise us. As we follow along the history of governments and of the human mind during the previous age, we expect it; we feel it is inevitable; we wait the bolt; we almost long for it—the bolt that is to beat down the insurgent impiety of nations, that is to punish the masters and teachers of mankind for their long abused trust, to avenge ages of wrong to humanity, and to vindicate the violated majesty of Heaven. Church and monarchy in Europe, had for centuries been running up a fearful account with God and man. We wait the bolt in awe and fear, but in assurance it will come, and when it falls we seem to hear the exult of the apocalypse, "We give Thee thanks, O Lord God Almighty, who wast, and art, and art to come, because Thou hast taken to Thyself Thy great power and hast reigned; and the nations were angry, and Thy wrath is come, and the time of the dead that they should be judged, and that Thou shouldst destroy them that destroy the earth."

Such was the prevalence and such some of the characteristics of the infidelity of the eighteenth century. If we were to attempt more specifically to characterize it, we should say its spirit was more essentially and intensely *anti-social* than *anti-Christian*—its fight more with facts than theories; more with the order of the world than even with its creed. Its skepticism was *social*, *ecclesiastical* and *political* even more than religious. Its primary impulse and passion were against Institutions. These more than dogmas—organisms more than principles, provoked, exasperated and oppressed it. Christianity was odious as the religion of church, state and society, even more than as the ordinance and revelation of God. Church, state and society, it hated as vast and oppressive facts. It hated God as their supposed guarantor. Its war was not on them for God's overthrow, but on Him as their champion. Though beginning in the theoretic and speculative, and entrenching and arming itself with the new philosophy, it grew to its terrible passion and power less as a dialectic, than a social birth, and was engaged more with economies than theologies. It was an insurrection of nations less against Christianity—which indeed had been veiled and caricatured to them—than against a spiritual power, calling itself of Christ, wrought through all the order of the world, and conservating and eternizing the most stupendous wrongs, lies and shames. It was on monstrous social and ecclesiastical disorders and corruptions it fed, in order to grow to its portentous strength and stature. It was these, far more than philosophic theses, that gave to it its passion and force.

This union of social with speculative skepticism will also account for many of the apparent contradictions. It was owing to this that it passed from disporting itself with the speculative and the abstract to a frantic war on the actual—that the jest and amusement of philosophers and the badinage and bon-mots of the savans, became the rage of the millions. It was because of the abuse of Christianity to the political and spiritual oppression of nations, that religious skepticism steps forth from a coterie of the salon to the field of arms, and from a controversy with scholastic subtleties grows to mortal combat with monarchy and hierarchy, and with society itself. Thus also beginning with theophilanthropic platitudes, it ends in blasphemies; with professions of fraternity it snares to massacre, and in the name of liberty and equality it erects the most terrific tyranny the earth ever saw.

With a prelusive cant of moralities, it sinks into the grossest sensualism and the vilest profligacy; the epigram and moral tableau give place to guillotines and bayonets; the carnival of the philanthropist changes to the carnage of fratricides; the

Tencins, and Deffands, and the Rolands are succeeded by the Dames des Halles; and the "*blanches nuits*" and Pagan orgies of the Regent are changed to the Jacobin club, the National Assembly, the conciergerie, and the tribunal of terror.

The *origin* and *focus*, the chief prevalence and the climacteric of this moral plague, were in the countries of the Romish communion, and in that country especially where despotism, spiritual and political, if not most absolute and complete, was at least most keenly felt, because it came in collision with the most advanced civilization, and the most stimulated and enlightened mind in Catholic Europe —France. It was in a country, where, in consequence, the atrocities, absurdities, and scandals of power, ecclesiastic and political, were most vividly appreciated and resented, that the plague first broke out.

It was at a period, too, in the history of that country when despotism was most offensive and irritating, because the sceptre of absolutism had passed from the mightiest and most brilliant of despots, to the hands of the most imbecile. The profligacy of hierarchy and monarchy provoked the bitterer as well as bolder hate, because impotency was now associated with arrogance.

It was a country, too, where through the alliance

of spiritual and political despotisms, a nominal Christianity had been made an accomplice of the unspeakable cruelties, and profligacies, and scandals of the hierarchy and monarchy for a thousand years, and which presented a history, which, if not the foulest and bloodiest in Europe, was the most so of all that had left to the nations, amid whom they had been enacted, life enough to perceive and resent them. The French Church was most offensive to the French mind, not because one was worst, or the other best, in Europe, so much as because in France there was exhibited a combination the highest possible of scandals and atrocities in one, with a subsisting vitality in the other.

CHAPTER II.

CAUSES OF THE INFIDELITY OF THE EIGHTEENTH CENTURY.

A century and a half precedent of Religious Passion and War; Relaxation, Exhaustion, and Reaction consequent—Position of the Religious Liberties of Nations at its close—Dethronement of the Religious Idea—Causes and Consequences—Religious Wars—Who was responsible for them and their Mischiefs to Faith—Aspect of the World at the opening of the Skeptical Era melancholy and portentous—Its Lessons.

Such was the great "Eclipse of Faith" in modern history. What was the cause, or what were the causes of this portentous phenomenon? Where lies the terrible responsibility? Is it with Protestantism? The cant of a certain school charges it there—a cant so often repeated that we suppose it has come to stand in the eyes of its utterers as an established historic fact; though, as far as we are aware, from the beginning hitherto, it has been mere allegation without proofs. It is contradicted not only by the philosophy of the case, drawing conclusions from the essential principles and tendencies of Protestantism, but moreover by the most patent facts, viz.: the origin, early foci, and the geographic theatre of the plague, as also by the ecclesiastic relations of nations amid whom it raged earliest, longest, and most violently, and where its deadly consequences continue most abundant this hour. These certainly do not point to Protestantism.

We do not, therefore, rush immediately to the opposite conclusion, that its cause was Romanism. Association is not necessarily causation. Nor is simplicity of cause to be expected of a phenomenon so vast, complex, and multiform. Its cause or causes will not probably be found exclusively with any one church, school, or country. The cause of causes, looming up in goblin hideousness, pre-eminent we believe, will appear to have been *spiritual despotism.* But this cause is Protean and cosmopolite. It has other capitals besides the Eternal City, and will produce its natural evil fruit, wherever found. The church also is armed with political power and State establishments, in other than Catholic countries; and this alliance will produce its disastrous consequences in Prussia and England as well as in Austria and France. Many minor causes we shall expect to find conspiring to the result. Of these in our present brief inquiry, we shall attempt an analysis only of those most prominent and of most significance for our times.

And first among these, I advert to a cause that

like a malignant atmosphere embraces and stimulates to abnormal viciousness and energy all others, nourishing all morbid growths; sinking the vital power, and giving an epidemic virulence to all the moral distemperatures of the times; I refer to a general condition of the European mind. It was a period of atony and exhaustion in the moral constitution of society; one of those times of relaxed and feeble tone, in which diseases and cancerous growths naturally set in.

What may be fitly termed the Skeptical Era in modern history opens with reaction against one hundred and fifty years of exalted religious sentiment, passion, and agonism. It was the collapse after four generations of religious wars—the low stage following the fever. It borders immediately on the great heroic and martyr era of modern history; an era colossal in its ideas and its passions, its virtues and its crimes; often blinded and misguided, yet ever intensely sincere and severe, and great even in its errors; whose faith now mounted to enthusiasm and vision, now sunk to a lurid and fiery fanaticism, but was ever a real and living faith;—whose seriousness not seldom hardened to austerity, and whose solemnity at times deepened to gloom; but there was heroism in its austerity and a grandeur in its gloom. It had seemed as if the human theatre, solemn with vaster than earthly figures and mundane interests, were lifted amid the awful light and shade of another world—a light and shade streaming across it like the unearthly glare or gloom in a landscape of Salvator, thrown across the earth from masses of black and broken thunder-cloud floating in a fiery ether. The tremendous drama enacted, with its titanic *personæ*, its vast forms of Empire, its stupendous destinies, its mighty actors, its Charles V., Francis II., Elizabeth, Philip II., the Duke of Orange, Ferdinand II., Wallenstein, Luther, Loyola and the like, grouped in a battle whose question compassed the fiery deep and the sapphire throne—such scenes and interests passing before them had, for almost a century and a half, kept the religious sentiment of the world to the tone of tragic passion, almost of agony. But to a cycle of such preternatural exaltation and tension, relaxation and subsidence were inevitable. Accordingly, immediately succeeding it, we enter an era of reactionary and divergent movement in the world's mind. Like Milton's Satan emerging from hell-gates, history leaves the hot and lurid air of fanatic passion, to sink ten thousand fathoms deep at once in chill mephitic damp and vapor.

By that law of action and reaction exhibited through all history, the world's mind now oscillates from intense earnestness and excitement to a frivolous apathy, a flippant and sneering indifference. Austerity had relaxed into dissoluteness, heroïsm had dissolved into a fastidious sybaritism. The tragedy had had its catastrophe, the comedy and the farce now enter. From the Baltic to the Mediterranean, and from the Vistula to the Atlantic, in the court and throughout the realms of the Stuarts and the Bourbons, the Hohenzollerns, the Hapsburgs and the Romanoffs, there seemed a transition from the Sampson Agonistes to the Comus. It was the revel of Circe after the battle of the Gods. The spirit of the Age was most unheroic, egotistical and godless. In the atmosphere of such a period skepticism could not fail to have rapid growth and diffusion. Every cause tending to produce it must have been stimulated to peculiar malignancy and power.

But not simply through the moral atony and collapse which followed it, was the great religious agonism of the world during the sixteenth and seventeenth centuries the cause of the infidelity of the period subsequent. Its woes had bred disgust; its crimes had produced revulsion; its inconsistencies provoked incredulity, and its fanaticism, abhorrence. Its atrocities and fatuities in the name of God and Religion had tended to make both a jest or a horror to the millions; and finally its issue being a drawn battle, establishing among the nations toleration from necessity, legitimating per force as between the European family of States, a dissent that was regarded as treason against Heaven, had begotten indifference from very impotency and despair. But on the other hand, while establishing as *between* nations tolerance from impotence, *within* nations the issue of that great struggle exhibits spiritual despotism in the form most adapted to breed incredulity and hate, viz. denuded of the defences of logic or sentiment and stripped of the prestige of universality, the associate of petty or local tyrannies, and upheld by mere mercenary military force. No wonder the logic of standing armies startled rather than tranquillized the faith of mankind, nor that mankind began to suspect that was hardly a kingdom of Truth that was upborne by a million of bayonets.

The great convulsion of the Reformation, which from the reign of Charles V. to the close of the Thirty Years War presents the religious idea as dominant in the politics of Europe, controlling its cabinets, agitating and swaying its millions and dashing nations together in the shock of arms, exhibits at its close neither of the great religious parties victorious, but each acquiescing of necessity in the existence and national independency of the other. The bloody gulf that had swallowed thirty millions of the human race is at last closed by the treaty of Westphalia. This political and religious settlement of Europe, leaves its nations in an armed truce. Vast military monarchies now appear on the map of Christendom, and these everywhere associated with state churches. The broken autocracy of the papacy crystallizes into national hierarchies. The fallen sceptre of the pontificate is grasped by the hand of primate or monarch. Nations are ecclesiastically independent of each other; but the millions crushed down under the double despotism of monarch and prelate, are kept down by mercenary myriads of bayonets. To them the religious independence of nations only aggravates and exasperates the sense of spiritual oppression.

Many causes now conspire to make the religious idea descend from its sovereignty over European history. That of wealth and of military aggrandizement now for one hundred and fifty years rise to the ascendency in the cabinet politics of Europe. Speculative thought meanwhile descends from the surface of affairs to mine for ages in the deeps below society, and under all the visible order of the world; or it subtilizes and soars away to the fields in the upper Ether, in the dim and distant regions of abstract to brew aloof from the present, storms for the future; there to weave and plight and paint those shifting phantasms of glittering haze and fiery vapor that shall descend on the coming time in the thunder-cloud and the tempest.

The causes of the dethronement of the religious idea from European history were various. Some of them as shedding light on the era and the question we investigate, we will note in passing.

And, *First.* The exhaustion, in the long agonism of society, of the passions and sentiments which made the religious idea sovereign and absolute. The limiting law of all intense excitement had obtained. The preternatural tension could not last for ever. The fever was spent, the fire had burned itself out. A reaction towards religious indifference and towards other interests and passions, was natural.

Second. The utter hopelessness of the strife which the rule of the religious Idea in politics necessitated. Universal ecclesiastical victory and empire were evidently impossible for either of the combatants. The struggle had of itself created mighty Protestant states. Prussia and the Netherlands had sprung forth full-armed at their birth, to battle and to victory. And must the fight now hopeless, be eternal? Evidently then another idea must take possession of the politics of the world; and that of religion, like all dethroned monarchs, could pass from sovereignty only to insignificance and contempt, or to imprisonment, exile or execution.

Third. Another cause was the severance for the time of the Papacy, from the council chamber of European politics. She had refused her accession to the treaty of Westphalia, because of the seculariza-tion of Prussia guarrantied by that settlement of Europe. Of course she could arrogate no tutelage or guardianship of an adjustment of Christendom against which she protested, and which she persisted to ignore. She was necessarily without influence in a system to which she refused to be a party. Her protest thus isolated her among the nations and reduced her for the time to political insignificancy and impotence. But it was her arrogation of leader-ship in European politics, and her ambition, chiefly, that had given the ascendency to the politico-reli-gious idea in Europe. The agonism of nations was antagonism against her usurpation. Zeal, often the product of danger, passes often with it.

Fourth. Compulsory endurance of dissent for a century and a half had abated the horror with which it was regarded at first, and begot a species of tolerance of it. No fire from heaven, and no strange curse overtook those whose creed was sup-posed to make them hated of God and cursed for both worlds. Men learned tolerance from familia-rity and from the apparent tolerance of heaven. But with the ignorant and superstitious, intolerance is wont to be exchanged only for indifference, and bigotry, for irreligion. There were other causes in particular countries, which we may not here notice particularly: *e. g.*, in England there was reaction against Puritan austerity, and the fanaticism of religious arms. The restoration of the Stuarts, with its dissoluteness and pusillanimity, had succeeded to the iron Protectorate, the stern grandeur of the Commonwealth and the martyr age of the First Charles; and subsequently the persiflage and libertinism of Queen Anne's court followed, with a brief interval only of more heroic temper, at the accession of William of Orange.

France exhibited the relaxation consequent on the long convulsion of her religious and civil wars. The revel and intrigue of the oriental seraglio had succeeded to the heroic age of Henry IV. and Coligny. The stake, the dagger of the assassin, and royal perjury had done their work. The Huguenots were sleeping in bloody graves, or had borne their wrongs and hatred to foreign climes. The national mind fell back into languor, frivolity, and indifference.

In Spain and Italy there was no longer the earnestness of a struggle against Protestantism. The Inquisition had done its work. From the Alps and the Pyrenees to the Mediterranean all was silent. Free thought was smothered in blood. Security, relaxation, corruption, and national decay were following.

Germany was prostrate, bleeding from the thirty years war: her youth consumed; whole climes desosolate, and becoming again haunts of wild beasts. The bones of her most gifted and heroic sons strew the fatal battle-field from the Baltic to the Rhine, the Alps and the Danube, and her very civilization is beaten back half a century. Exhaustion and the low stage have succeeded to the fever. Moreover, throughout Europe generally, the mercantile and economical interest of nations, which now becomes an ascendant one, requires new political combinations irrespective of religious predilections and affinities: *e. g.*, the combinations around Louis XIV. were independent of the question of religious schools. Each religious sect and party, Greek, Latin, Papal, Protestant, Turk, or Frank, are grouped in shifting confederation irrespective of ecclesiastical affinities.

From all these causes a new spirit comes to the helm of affairs. The clangor of religious arms that has resounded through a terrible century, ceases. The storm of war that had wandered like a fury through every country of Europe from the British Isles to the Adriatic, is at length laid. The nations no more slay each other in the name of the God of

Peace. But the curses of that strife still linger, not only in the desolation of the fairest portions of Europe, its sacked cities, wasted realms, ruined culture, and demoralized civilization; not only in the natural subsidence of the mind of nations into religious indifference from both the exhaustion and hopelessness of their effort at religious empire; but in disgust with religion itself, as connecting itself with the peculiar atrocities and cruelties, the fanaticisms and hypocrisies of the religious wars.

All wars are demoralizing; but the religious are most corrupting of all wars. They are of all, most ruthless or cruel: you pursue your enemy in them, not merely as your foe, but as a miscreant accursed of heaven. Why should you show mercy where your creed tells you God himself shows none? You outlaw him from human sympathy, and drive him from the number of men. He already ranks to you with the infernals. The personal enemy now is exalted to an avenger of heaven. Private revenge, cupidity, and ambition, become consecrated as a zeal for God. You avenge your own braved intolerance and wounded pride as insults to the Divine Majesty. There is, therefore, in such wars the least of moderation or mercy. Conscience lays down its watch; passion gluts itself without restraint, and the lusts of hell receive the sanction of heaven. A creed, a metaphysical formulary, perhaps, is enough now to baptize cruelties which unsophisticated nature regards as purely devilish. I need not stop to argue that such wars must of themselves lead to infidelity, when the madness of the hour is passed, if men dare to think. First, they must breed this with manifold other curses in the corruption they engender. Again, what can sooner teach rejection of a creed than to see it made the warrant for sordid lust and horrid crimes? What sooner compel me to disbelieve in God altogether than seeing Him made the patron of wickedness? You array my moral nature against Him. My immortal instincts arise and protest: "Thou, O God, art of purer eyes than to behold iniquity." No other God will they receive. They drive me to infidelity when they make religion to sanction revenge and cruelty.

No wonder, then, that Europe, with the page of a century and a half of religious wars before it, read therein a lesson of infidelity and of disgust with a faith in whose name such horrors were perpetrated. Nor is it a wonder, that with such antecedents, there was in the mind of the age corruption in which these lessons might readily take root.

All these causes tended to produce a general reaction in the European mind towards indifference and unbelief. There was, therefore, a general relaxation of Christendom consequent on its long and intense paroxysm, a relaxation both in religious sentiment and the general tone of society. The States of Europe rushed into the game of wealth. Then were courts immersed in schemes of economy, trade, and finance, or in oriental voluptuousness and seraglio intrigue; and the Papacy, meanwhile, sinking back again from the spasm of severer morality and ecclesiastic reform to which antagonism to Luther had scourged it, returned to its old dissoluteness of manners, its avarice, corruption, and nepotism.

To all these causes impelling Christendom to the verge of an era of irreligion, must be added the indifference naturally bred of the aspect of various forms of dissent, living newly side by side in each other's presence; just as the strictness of moral principle in great cities is often impaired by the very multitude and familiarity of practices violative of it, which one is compelled to witness. He that is newly wonted to see his faith and his principles denied and trampled under foot of multitudes, is in danger of losing his own reverence and belief in regard to them.

Finally we must reckon amid causes of skepticism the confusion of ideas inevitable on such a great breaking up of the world's mind as the Lutheran

Reformation, producing "distress of nations with perplexity."

We refer to these causes as general ones, giving increased virulence to other great agencies, which I shall hereafter notice, in plunging the world into infidelity.

Such were the ages precedent to the skeptical era, such the times of its preparation and inauguration. It was, as we have seen, a bloody cancer on a world spent with a century and a half of Religious carnage. It was the Pale Horse of the Apocalypse following the Red, and Hell was in its train.

But before we leave this topic we pause and ask who is responsible—who is rightfully arraigned at the bar of History for these horrible religious wars and their baleful influence on religious belief? That power, we are compelled to answer, whose attempted tyranny over belief caused them, provoked, compelled and perpetuated them, who would not allow to the nations the natural rights of free faith and free worship without them—Rome. The ruffian that attempts to bind my hands and put out my eyes, or to keep me down and fettered when I am fallen, he is responsible and not I, for the blood that may flow in my attempts to deliver and defend myself.

A power sat in Rome claiming the empire of the world, and there could be no peace on earth until she should be compelled to veil or at least keep in abeyance that assumption. It took a century and a half of war and crime, and the exhaustion of the nations of Europe, to secure that result. Back then of those bloody ages—pouring forth from the gates of the Vatican as from the ever-open gates of Janus of old, the horrid plague of war on Europe—sits as cause, the Pontifical City. For these wars, and the woes and crimes and impiety and infidelity they wrought, she must bear the first responsibility at the bar of History and of God. Her theory—her principle of intolerance and assumption of the spiritual empire of Christendom and of the right of the secular sword—necessitated those wars. History, too, must record that often her practice—her ambition and intrigue, fanaticism and conspiracy against nations and dynasties—drove the nations into them. So far, then, as those ages of religious wars were the cause of infidelity, not Protestantism surely but her antagonist, is primarily responsible.

Such was Rome's preëminence and priority of position in regard to this long and sanguinary struggle. Not that she was always in each instance the first aggressor, nor that intolerance and persecution attached to her alone, nor that Protestant arms were always guiltless or unstained by atrocities. Alas! the fury of Religious arms once admitted, the cup of blood once tasted, none can answer for the horrors that may ensue in the intoxication that follows. Neither party can look back on those ages and say I am guiltless. Both may say, "verily we have thought we were doing God service in wasting accursed nations." We should judge men in the light of their own age—charitably. We should judge principles in the light of all ages—strictly and severely.

We have thus considered and described the *fact* we are attempting to analyze—the defection of the human mind from Christianity in the last century, and the general condition of the world's mind when it appeared. The era of skepticism opens with the moral constitution of the world relaxed, and its life-pulse beating heavy and feeble. Its tone is low; the vital principle faint. It is a time for disease to set in. The guardian forces of the social system are asleep. Its energies of resistance are paralyzed and the elements of corruption are at work; a dissolution is begun. We feel, as we enter the period in question, that we approach some melancholy catastrophe of human society; one of those sad, chill, feeble, foul epochs which mark the decay and death of nations and civilizations. Its type of life and passion is worn out, and itself in collapse. Chivalry, honor, heroism and faith lie dying; the mean and crawling vices—the worms of dissolution begin to appear. The world seems old and wan. The air grows chill, the gloom thickens. We feel we are entering the *penumbra of the eclipse* and the occultation of the orb of light and warmth is at hand. Thus the skepticle cycle impresses us as it enters. But there are also in its aspect portents of change. Society is torpid, spent, faint. But we may prophesy for it, there is fever lurking in that ague stage, and madness and delirium are couched in that atony. It is a world where all things seem portentous. We snuff the plague in that stagnant air. We feel death in its chill and its gloom. We feel the shadow of the destroying angel on that sky. We momently wait his epiphany. That sky we feel is to kindle to another hue. Blood-red it rises before us, and beneath it twenty millions of victims. We hear the edict "these millions for the guillotine; these for sword; for famine and pestilence and the rage of the elements these; and these for madness and terror and sorrow and shame." There is a tumult of nations raging against God. The abyss yawns under European civilization, and Hell from beneath is stirred to meet the mighty, the gifted, the brave, the beautiful, the noble, at their coming. "*Thou beheldest and drove asunder the nations.—The deep uttered his voice, and lifted up his hands on high—*

At the light of thine arrows they went and at the shining of thy glittering spear—So perish all thine enemies, Oh Jehovah."

But before the earth is ripe for that vintage, this low tone in the world's life must pass to a paroxysm of fanatic atheism, or at least of infidelity raging against Christianity. We have hereafter to inquire through what causes eminently, and in what form that baleful epidemic of unbelief broke forth on such an era as we have described and overspread the earth.

But one lesson of solemn import the precursive view we have taken of our theme, teaches us.

As we close our present survey of this melancholy chapter of History we are awed with the sense of a Nemesis, celestial or infernal, on the track of nations. The night-shade of infidelity that waved over a cycle sprang from thirty millions of graves. The crimson carnival of revolution only alternated with and avenged the auto-da-fé of a world.

Would that Christendom might learn from this sad lesson how wretched, futile and guilty is force for the extension of religion! Whoso opens the seals of a religious war unlocks the bottomless pit: he lets loose a devil upon earth, whose chaining none may foreknow.

Let us be thankful that we live in the light of a

later period in history, and let us look at the actors in the melancholy drama in review, often with pity for their errors, and admiration for their heroism, but detestation, never too strong for their principles and their policy in the arbitrament of questions of religious faith. And let us not forget, that in their position, and in the light of their age, we not improbably had been equally guilty.

I was about to congratulate you that the gulf of religious wars is closed. But I must restrain my gratulation. I hear this very hour the clangor of innumerable arms brandished in religious pretence, if not in phrensy. From the Nubian sands to the Polar snows, from the Caucasus to the Atlantic, I hear the hum of nations mustering to carnage in the name of God and religious faith, as well as of Empire. Like a baleful meteor religious fanaticism flames over the advancing hosts, mingling and baptizing other passions. A war of religion seems again opened, and tidings from the rising sun are telling us the old devil is again unchained, walking the shores of the Euxine or flapping his red wing o'er its wave.

I restrict my gratulations. Rather with warmer gratitude let us thank God that we live in a country where religious tolerance is not a right wrested from despots with a bloody hand, but seemingly as natural to our land as our rivers and our mountains—a *first truth*, a *life principle* in our *civilization*—a tolerance not of *indifference*, or *unbelief*, or of *compromise*, or *suppression* of principle, but a tolerance where perfect freedom of thought and speech breaks the edge of religious hatred, and keeps religious passions from out-breaking violence and secret conspiracy, by furnishing them expression and scope in a fair and open field of argument—such a field as alone truth asks—the free lists of reason and speech.

May heaven ever keep those lists open. The hand, the sect, the party that in any part of these lands shall attempt to close them—let all the people curse it. Historic ages shall send down their *Amen*. Let us never fear to leave our Christian faith in those lists with truth and God, the human mind, and the sacred Spirit. Fiercely as may rage the conflict, with these arbiters and champions in the strife, a true faith need never fear. Its banner shall float for ever in our skies. If in such a field it falls, it will be because faith and liberty have no longer place on the earth. But living or dying, their fate is one. Of one birth, one cradle, one history, one faith, and one freedom—if fall they must, they shall fall on the same field, shrouded in the same bloody banner, and be buried in the same grave.

CHAPTER III.

REVOLUTION IN PHILOSOPHY.

Revolution in Philosophy—A necessity of Social Progress perverted by Spiritual Despotism to the destruction of Faith—Protestantism a Revolutionist in Philosophy—Different Philosophic Methods —Aristotelian—Scholastic—Baconian—Mediæval Philosophy, the instrument of Spiritual Despotism—Aristotle and the Pope, Joint Monarchs and High Priests of thought and faith—Revolution in Philosophy, an emancipation of mind—Its position in the Map of Modern History—Eras of Religious, Philosophical, and Political Revolution—Futility and fruitlessness of the Old Philosophy—A barren toil in an endless circle—A blind and fetter of Mind—Its Overthrow a Necessity—Why it dragged Faith with it in its Fall—Different Results in different Countries—Disasters to Faith, the result of Spiritual Despotism—Protestantism as Revolutionist in Philosophy a mighty Benefactor—Plea of the Baconian Philosophy.

In previously discussing the skepticism of the seventeenth and eighteenth centuries, we have endeavored to exhibit its wide prevalence, some of its distinctive characteristics, and the condition of the world in which it broke out and spread; or in other words, the extent, type, and *predisposing* causes, of that great moral plague.

We have now to consider a great fact in European history, which may be termed an *occasional cause;*

that is, one not in itself competent to the result, but having such efficiency only from the accidental coincidence and co-operation of other causes. We refer to the great Revolution in Philosophy, that inaugurated the world's transition from mediæval to modern history—a revolution usually dated and named from Lord Bacon, of the latter half of the sixteenth century, although he is not so much the author as elucidator, and instaurator of the philosophy that bears his name.

The Baconian method is older than Bacon—as old, indeed, as mind. It began with the education of the first human soul. But its enunciation, exposition, and application by Lord Bacon, more especially in the department of physics, as afterwards by Des Cartes in metaphysics, unquestionably mark a signal epoch in the history of philosophy; and they were followed directly by a movement so rapid, potent, and radical, in the thinking and scientific world, that we term it a philosophical *revolution*. This revolution synchronizes with another great movement in the European mind—the Lutheran Reformation—to which it stands also logically related both as cause and effect. Indeed, the Reformation may be considered as one compartment of the vast field—one act in the mighty drama of that philosophic revolution, that beginning with the first truths and primal intuitions of the mind, was destined to sweep in its scope the whole universe of life and action.

The enemies of the emancipation of intellect and faith, charge on the religious reform of the sixteenth century, that it produced the religious skepticism of the eighteenth, by adopting as its logical instrument the new philosophical method—that it begat the philosophical revolution, and, through it, the infidelity associated with it. But of that disastrous result, it was, in truth, only the *occasional cause;* having its evil efficiency to that result, only from other causes; such as the low and feeble tone in the moral constitution of the world, and the reaction, exhaustion, and collapse following ages of a preternatural exaltation of the religious sentiment, and of the phrenzy of religious arms. That revolution was in itself beneficent and healthful and one necessary to the world's progress; and it was productive of irreligion, only as the cool and bracing air may produce fever in the debilitated body, or as the genial and vital warmth may induce corruption in a corpse. But as especially infecting it with a morbific and malignant tendency we have to note *spiritual despotism*—a cause essentially *efficient* of the sad consequence—intrinsically, eternally, universally malignant; certain under all circumstances where it shall not absolutely stifle mind to syncope or death, to make it unbelieving or misbelieving.

In pursuance, therefore, of our general theme, we propose now to discuss this revolution in philosophy, in its relations to the skepticism contemporary and subsequent, and, as far as it was a cause of that phenomenon, to inquire *why* it was so, and *who* is *responsible* for its being so.

But first let us endeavor to give a clear idea of what we mean by a *revolution in philosophy*. No feature of the period we are considering is more important to be noted or rightly understood.

By a "Revolution in Philosophy" we mean a *change in our methods of investigation or proof—a change in the primary laws and process of reasoning and in our grounds* of belief.

There are two methods by which questions may be tried or a thing examined—one, is by looking at the thing itself, its nature, properties, elements, causes, effects, relations. The other, is by turning over the pages of authority; by inquiring what somebody else has said or determined on the subject. The former method is the ANALYTIC, which proceeds by taking things to pieces, and by examining their intrinsic qualities and relations. The latter is the DOGMATIC, which proceeds by inquiring after the dogmas or the pronounced judgments and transmitted decisions of others. The latter method obtained throughout Europe in whatever claimed to be science, in the ages before Luther and Bacon, indeed through the mediæval period; *i. e.* for more than one thousand years.

The philosophy that arose based on this method was called *Aristotelian*, not because Aristotle uses or teaches the dogmatic method. No philosopher of the ancient, or, we may say, even of the modern world, ever used the analytic or inductive mode, more freely or more successfully than that one of the subtlest, most comprehensive, and most analytic of human intellects.

The mediæval philosophy was called Aristotelian, because it referred to Aristotle's teachings in logic, rhetoric, ethics, physics, etc., as the finished authoritative Bible of human knowledge—the accomplished possible of science—the perfected encyclopædia of results attainable by the human intellect.

It was called *scholastic*, from the scholastics or schoolmen; a class of dialecticians, mostly theologians and ecclesiastics, which appeared in the dark ages, and which constructed out of Aristotle's philosophy, a logic which became the great defence of the Papacy. It placed indeed the Pagan, Greek and the Latin Pontiff, as joint monarchs, on the same philosophical throne. The Pope and Aristotle were its associate high priests; the dialectics of the Stagyrite and the decretals of the Pontiff constituted the joint supreme oracle of human thought. Out of the subtle analysis, divisions, definitions and classifications of the acute Greek, the schoolmen had framed a dialectic, whose formularies were only a manual of logical traps, nets, tricks, and snares, that snapped you up unawares into the admission of absurdities the most palpable; schemes of casuistic fence, of cut, thrust, feint and parry; a system of intellectual legerdemain, that juggled you out of belief in your own eyes and ears, into acceptance of dogmas conflicting never so strongly with the common sense and irresistible instinctive judgment of the mind. It had become a mere science of quibble, of sophistical subtleties, of words without things, and reasoning without knowledge of the subject matter. This philosophy aiding the church, had in turn been consecrated by it. They upheld each other and were bound together. Thus the spiritual power representing Christianity had bound this philosophy as a chain around the mind of the world.

So it was till the sixteenth century. The revolution in philosophy was the breaking of this chain—the substitution of the analytic or inductive method in place of the scholastic. Of this revolution Bacon and Des Cartes are the great leaders in the realm of philosophy; Luther in his reform, was its practical asserter in the domain of religion. The assertion of the right of private judgment and of the duty of the individual Christian to prove all things, necessarily overthrew the old philosophy and faith together.

This Baconian or Cartesian method, thus vindicated, is to this day an abhorrence in the eyes of Rome. The old philosophy still lingers ghostlike around her universities, waiting the full day-break to flee. The nations that seized on the new method and applied it, have gone forward in power at least—power in the world of thought, in science, reason, invention, administrations and power over the material world, such as presents them almost as a superior order of beings compared with the nations which have rejected it.

But this intellectual emancipation produced the mingled effects which liberty must in a world like ours. It unquestionably became abused to license and skepticism. In casting away Aristotle and Pope, men unquestionably did often proceed to cast away Jesus Christ, and in revolt against the authority of Rome, they cast away also allegiance to Christianity itself.

The question now is, who is responsible for this? or rather is Protestantism, as often charged, the guilty cause of it? Protestantism rejects all authority in matters of religious faith but the word of God. Is she responsible because some, adopting the same philosophic method, in casting away Papal decretals and Canon law, cast the Bible away with them?

Macauley thus speaks of the alliance between Aristotle's philosophy and the church, with the consequences. "In the fifth century Christianity had conquered Paganism, and Paganism had enfeebled Christianity. The rites of the Parthenon passed into the worship of the Church; the subtleties of the academy, into her creed. Similar trifles just as subtle, interminable and unprofitable, occupied the sharp intellects of the schoolmen. At length the time had come when the barren philosophy which had worn so many shapes, mingled with so many creeds, had survived empires, religions, races, languages, was destined to fall. Driven from its ancient haunts, it had taken sanctuary in that church which it at first had persecuted; and like the daring fiends of the poet

> "Placed its seat
> Next to the seat of God,
> And with its darkness durst affront His light."

Words, mere words, nothing but words had been the fruit of all the toil of all the most renowned sages of sixty generations. "In an evil day," says Bacon, "though with great pomp and solemnity, was the ill-starred alliance stricken between the Old Philosophy and the New Faith." Ill-starred in truth it was. For the time was to come when it was to hang like a vast-decayed column from the temple it was to support, threatening to drag the whole structure with it to the dust. It was a coat of mail, destined to become a compress, preventing or distorting the growth, and finally stifling life. It was an alliance of the corruptible with the incorruptible, the mortal with immortality, destined surely to beget misbelief or unbelief. When one should die, as die it must, it would seem to draw the other into the same grave with it, as the body the soul. Disastrous consequences to Faith in Christianity itself could not fail to ensue, when the canonized falsity should be exploded, and the philosophy baptized as of God and consecrated as His ordinance, should be exposed as a barren mockery. But I ask, is the party that tears away the mockery or the one that vouches for its substantiality, responsible for those mischiefs of its exposure?

Nothing is more common in certain quarters than to deplore or accuse the Protestant Reformation as the cause, through the new philosophic method, of the infidelity of the eighteenth century and its closing Revolutionary catastrophe. It has become the cant of a school, not only of professed Romanists, but of pseudo-Protestant writers; repeated so often, that not only themselves believe it, but timid Protestants have begun often to distrust and fear their own principles.

An investigation of the case brings home the charge to the accusers themselves. We believe it can be shown it was the despotism attempted by the spiritual power over the human mind—by Rome —that was the cause that the change in philosophizing, which was requisite to the progress of humanity, became a ruinous revolution instead of a gradual and conservative reform; that she necessitated such a result by her treatment of the minds of Europe, in the previous ages of her despotism over the West. It was a necessity of civilization *through her act.* But whether regarded or not as a necessity of civilization, it was at least the great social achievement of the era we are considering—a vast step in actual progress, though bearing, it may be, through abysses.

To aid our apprehension of the important relations of this topic, let us look at its position on the map of modern history.

Modern history from 1500 to the present divides itself into three great periods, according to the ideas that rule history during those periods, and around which gather their vital struggle and central interest; viz. the periods of Religious, Philosophical and Political Revolutions. Dating modern history from 1500 or the beginning of the Lutheran Reformation, the first period extends thence to 1648 or the treaty of Westphalia. The second, from the treaty of Westphalia (1648), to the French Revolution (1790). The third, from the opening of the French Revolution to the present. The great struggle of the first period is in the religious or ecclesiastical, of the second in the philosophical, the third in the political realm.

The great question of the first, from 1520 to 1648, related to the *source, nature*, and *organization*, of *spiritual authority and rule;* in the second (from 1648 to 1790), to the *fundamental principle* and *philosophical method of all knowledge and belief.* In the third (1790 to the present), to the *political constitution and order*, which should be the outward embodiment and representative of the inward sentiments and convictions of society—*the visible realization in institutions* of *the world's thought and belief.* Each of these steps or processes is as necessary to the series in the great logic of civilization—each a segment of the same great stream, but each with its own peculiar direction, impediments, rapids and cataracts.

The great work of the second period (1648–1790)

that we are now considering, summed up in its beneficent results, was the emancipation of the human mind in the realm of philosophy—the overthrow of the Aristotelian, or more properly, the scholastic, and the establishment of the Baconian or analytic method in all reasoning. Or in other words, it was the legitimation in society of the inductive process and the right of private judgment, in all belief.

Both the above methods, the dogmatic and inductive, in their sphere are legitimate—either transcending its sphere is pernicious. Where God has placed a thing before me in my view and within my grasp, analysis is an obvious command of reason and of God. Where things are beyond my vision and knowledge, I must receive them on authority and testimony if I receive them at all. And where my reason accepts a record as from God, my reason also binds me to accept as true what is therein stated. But it is obviously as unphilosophic to call in theologic authorities to settle for us, questions lying out of the scope of revelation, and in that of mere human discovery, as, *e. g.*, those of astronomy, or mechanics, or chemistry, as it would be to attempt to determine the high mysteries of the invisible world and facts of divine government, by geometry, algebra and the astronomic analysis; and he errs as much, who essays to determine whether the earth is the centre of the universe, and the sun revolves around it, or vice versa, by consulting canon law and papal bulls, as he who should think to call down Gabriel to work out for him a problem in trigonometry. I have no more right to ask God to do for me what He has given me power to do for myself, than I have to reject statements He has graciously been pleased to make of truths infinitely and for ever above my mortal ken.

But in the sixteenth century, the philosophy of authority had far transcended its legitimate bounds and grasped in its prerogative all departments of human knowledge. In the name of an infallible authority imparted of Heaven, the Church had applied the clamps and meshes of a subtle scholasticism, calling itself of Aristotle, to all science; had usurped the prerogative of all truth, and put the universal human mind under censorship: a man might be burned as readily for a thesis in astronomy, as in theology; for the heresy of the Copernican system, as for a denial of transubstantiation. Authority was called in to settle everything. Aristotle's categories and dialectics wedded to Papal prerogative—these formed a prison closure round the world, beyond which reason or inquiry became not only absurd, but impious.

"Looking at the philosophy of modern times,"

says Morell in his History of Philosophy, "in connection with that which for nearly two thousand years had preceded it, we see it bearing the marks of an independence, which since the days of Plato and Aristotle had been altogether unknown. The scholastic ages in particular were marked by a well-nigh slavish deference to authority—an authority which was balanced with some degree of equality between Aristotle on the one hand, and the Pope on the other. Philosophy during this period was content not only to be held in leading-strings, but to be nurtured and instructed by dogmatic theology as an obedient child, by its parent or guardian. It was timid in all its movements, feeble in its effects, and felt so much need of extraneous support that it willingly sanctioned an appeal to those who, the one in the ancient, the other in the modern world, had succeeded in gaining the confidence and subduing the reason of mankind."

"The Reformation was a revolt against authority, and presented the spectacle of the human reason once more asserting its independence, and indignantly bursting the chains by which it had so long been bound; for whether we regard the movement which then took place, in the religious, the political, or philosophical world, they are alike characterized by the same determination to shake off the trammels of servitude to which the will of humanity had for many past ages submitted. It was in the sixteenth century (the Reformation) that authorities which had been long doubted were openly disavowed, that the first overthrow of intellectual and spiritual despotism was given and received."

This great achievement of the Reformation was not only due to the free genius which pervaded it, but to its ecclesiastic revolt from the Pope—one of the great masters or authorities to which scholasticism professed allegiance—and especially to its bringing its appeal to the private judgment of all men, with the open Bible in hand, presenting its warrant for universal intellectual liberty in the command given not to Apostles and Popes, but the Christian Brotherhood, "prove all things, hold fast that which is good."

A Revolution in Philosophy was a necessity of European Civilization.—Society could not advance without it. The old organum—as the dialectic of the old philosophic school was termed—had become a mere fetter to humanity; inadequate to discover a new truth or to defend an old one, but simply to entangle and enchain mind—a mere idle, barren gymnastic, wearying minds with ceaseless gyrations and cunning manœuvre and evolution, but advancing never a step.

Nothing is more vital to society than a true philosophic method or primary law and process of belief. Nothing could be more fatal to real progress than the old method. It was futile, fruitless toil in endless circle. It was rolling the ever-rebounding stone of Sisyphus or pouring water in the bottomless urns of the Danaides. Was a proposition in physics or metaphysics to be determined? The school-men sent you not to analyze the thing, but they coerced it into the categories and syllabus of the subtle Greek; they put it into the strait-waistcoat of some dialectic formula; they put it upon the rack and torture of syllogism and enthymeme, and finally bound it down and smothered it by the decrees of Councils and the bulls of Popes. Was the inquirer still unsatisfied? The ponderous names of a Duns Scotus, a Thomas Aquinas, or some Seraphic Doctor, or some Gregory or Innocent or Boniface, were made to thunder about his ears with the technical barbarisms of a scholastic jargon, till overwhelmed and confounded, if not convinced, he was glad to be silent, especially as those barbarisms were no mere *bruta fulmina*, but behind them was brandished before his eyes the *ultima ratio* of spiritual despots—the mightier logic of imprisonment, wheel and fagot.

Ages of such processes manifestly led to nothing—certainly to no discovery or progress. The utterance of millions under force or fear could prove nothing, discover nothing. Indeed discovery and progress were not the aim of these processes. They were rather devices to keep down revolt against the intellectual duarchs that ruled the world. The whole aim was to keep all things fast bound where they were.

Again the talismanic secret of the old Logic—its wondrous power in the eyes of its professors was in its *forms—forms which could dispense with the substance of things* and with real knowledge, and *were in themselves a universal solvent for all questions, even of things themselves unknown*—forms so wonderful, that you could sit down in your study, and without telescope or celestial observation, cypher out the essences of the stars or the problems of the moon's life. The adept had arrived at such wonderful sleight of logical technic and formulary, that independent of all prior examination or knowledge, he could extort the truth out of any question, no matter how novel or mysterious, how occult, awful or fanciful. He could tell you with equal facility the population of Saturn, the number of feathers on the wing of the cherubim, and how many angels could stand on the point of a needle. Armed with these and in his own list, your true scholastic athlete was no common antagonist. He would snap up the wariest in his syllogistic gin; floor the doughtiest with some nimble fetch. Now he would distract you with his quick and subtle practice; now dazzle you with some glittering tenuous sophism; until he could thrust the blade of some keen technic through the joints of your harness. Now, Aristotle failing him, he would gore you unaware with some pontific bull; now brain you outright with some ecclesiastical canon. And if all this would not finish an adversary, then try the illumination of fire! burn him! or the wheel and scourge may awaken his logical consciousness, or at least the dungeon with its darkness and solitude and fastings, may ensure him sober and clear-brained leisure for reflecting on the arguments resisted. Indeed often the theologue and schoolman of the middle ages was in the logical lists an antagonist as formidable as was Nero in the Roman Circus, with the Pretorian Guard to back him, to the unhappy contestant for the honors of the fiddle.

Now the end of centuries of labor and conflict of this kind could only be words, words, words; mere words, save that their filmy and glittering maze was a blind and mesh to the mind of the world. Intellectual bewilderment, enslavement and stagnation could only ensue. Society could no more advance than Bulwer's man that thought to travel by endlessly gyrating on one leg. Progress by the old logic was, as if one were to attempt to go to New

York from St. Louis, by the way of the Mammoth Cave. Wind about as much as you would through dark or glittering labyrinth, over flood and cliff and through fairy grots or dim mysterious avenues, toil as you might over rough or smooth and steeps ascending or descending, you were certain at last to return on yourself and emerge where you started, near *Green River*.

A new direction for the intellect was needed; a change of fundamental principles and primal method in the investigation of truth or quest of knowledge, another "*organum*" or new instrument of reasoning. This was a primal want of society—the first step towards all sure and permanent progress. I must be assured my method of reasoning is right, or I may weary myself for ever without discovering a principle or ascertaining a fact. Society had for ages thus labored, adding not a single science and hardly a new art or even a new truth, for two thousand years. The trouble was not the want of genius or labor, but the method was vicious. A man will never climb Mont Blanc by working a treadmill, work he ever so vigorously. The world has wasted its strength in ever "revolving questions" as Macaulay calls them, on controversies ever recurring again, such as whether pain is an evil? whether all things are fated? whether we can be certain of anything?

whether we can be certain that we are certain of nothing, &c. Philosophy was battling over these questions in the age of Luther, as in the age of Socrates, and still no nearer the end of the treadmill. An endless round of sonorous nothings, technical barbarisms, casuistical subtleties, resounded in the ears of society as it plodded its weary way over "many a frozen, many a fiery Alp," mid rivers of inky blackness, or eddying flame and phantom peopled wildernesses, in endless mazes wandering; emulating in its bootless and ceaseless toil the fabled children of eternal night; till at last emerging from its dark sojourn, lo it finds itself just where it started weary centuries ago.

An emancipation of society from a Philosophy that thus imprisoned it, was obviously a necessity of progress. Its achievement from some source, was we think a certainty, as well as necessity of the ages, had there been no Bacon, no Des Cartes, no Luther.

We might then leave the charge against Protestantism, of causing infidelity through the philosophic method she vindicated and inaugurated, with the simple statement that *in this she was only the occasioning cause of a philosophic revolution, necessary and sure to come in some way, because the life of society required it.* But we do not choose to leave it there. Rather we accept the charge as a panegyric, rather we proudly claim, to her immortal honor, the glory of the intellectual emancipation of mankind, even with all the evils incident thereto.

But of this, more hereafter. We admit that Protestantism was an occasion, the great occasion, if you please, of the revolution in philosophy in the sixteenth and seventeenth centuries; a revolution, nevertheless, which, as a necessity of European civilization and progress, was sure from some cause to occur. The question still remains, what made a revolution thus necessary and inevitable, so disastrous to religious faith? What had so abused the name of religion before the nations, that the emancipation of thought must be an insurrection against God? had so abused the human reason, that it could not separate spiritual enslavement from submission to the authority of Heaven? and could see no pathway for society between drivelling superstition and blasphemous rejection of all religion? What power had made the darkness of its dungeon so dark, and for such ages, that when its prison-walls were broken, its victims became blinded by the very light? What power had so inwrought a sophistical and illusive philosophy with Christian truth, in the mind of the world, that you could not tear away that philosophy, without dragging down with it in ruins the temple of God? Who had so identified Christianity with the sterile system of the schoolmen, that the nations must remain in hopeless feebleness and puerility, or, as of old, become inventors only by becoming like the children of Cain? Certainly, beyond all other powers in Europe, she was responsible for this, who for one thousand years had claimed to be intellectual and spiritual lord of mankind.

I have said Protestantism was the *occasion* of that philosophic revolution. It was so, inasmuch as it stirred the intellectual deeps of Europe, and as it summoned mankind in insurrection against a spiritual despotism that had indissolubly bound up its authority with that of the scholastic philosophy, so that both must stand or fall together.

It was also obliged, in vindication of itself against spiritual despotism, to adopt, assert, and vindicate the new philosophy. It became, therefore, a great champion and monument of the Baconian method. So far, and no further, does it stand related as a cause, through it, to the infidelity of the sixteenth century.

It is not to be denied that the intellect of Europe, when emancipated, ran often into wild, eccentric, and ruinous ways. It would have been strange, had it not done so. The license of the emancipated is commonly in proportion to the severity of the despotism they have endured. This is ever one of the bitterest curses of despotism, and one that most unequivocally demonstrates its intrinsic and irremediable mischievousness. The atrocities and extravagances of liberty being thus the most damning accusation of the precedent despotism, how vehemently do those of the mind of Europe, after the emancipation of the Reformation, arraign the spiritual tyranny of previous ages! The infidelity of Protestant freedom, if a proved fact, would be the great opprobrium of the present Catholic despotism. But it is not so much the infidelity of Protestant freedom, as the indignant insurrection of mind in *Catholic* Europe against Christianity, that presents the darkest picture of the age we are considering.

It results from the necessary tendency of all transition periods also, that, in such an intellectual break-up of the world as that of the sixteenth and seventeenth centuries, abnormal and irregular manifestations of every kind were likely to appear. It is difficult for the human mind to stop in revolutions. When it begins to cast its false creeds and false gods overboard, it is apt also to throw away the true. This danger is incident to the abandonment of any antiquated and venerated error; of course, to all reform and all progress. The safety with which this danger is passed, depends *on the fidelity with which the spiritual and intellectual instructors and guardians of a people have previously discharged their trust.* There is what Morell calls "the skepticism of ignorance:" that is, the unbelief of a people, who, having their faith and veneration for a corrupt church and spurious Christianity destroyed, and having no knowledge of the genuine to supply their place, in their ignorance, rise in indignation and incredulous scorn against all religion. Such was that of large portions of Europe, and eminently that of France, in the eighteenth century. "Such," says Morell, speaking of this skepticism of ignorance, "is, to a great extent, the present state of France. Happily, the diffusion of religious truth is too general in England, to admit the return, except, indeed, under the most extraordinary circumstances, of another age of unbelief in the groundwork of man's natural religious sentiments." Morell here announces the cause and the cure of this species of unbelief. Imperfectly as the spiritual curators and teachers of Britain had discharged their trust, in consequence of her imperfect Protestantism, still enough of religious truth had been diffused to save her, amid the unbelief that like a storm swept Catholic France. If, on the overthrow of a false Christianity and philosophy by the Lutheran reform, the skepticism of ignorance entered, that power we are constrained to arraign, as chiefly responsible, that for one thousand years had been the intellectual and spiritual dictator of Europe, the high priest of its faith, worship, and philosophy—Rome. If we inquire where in Christendom the Baconian philosophy was most abused to the production of infidelity, and where first and chiefly it became the poisoner of the nations, where it was perverted to the organ of a war on heaven, and an elaborator of infernal arms, and where it equipped the mightiest actors, and achieved the most hideous triumphs in that impious conflict, we are pointed at once to the countries of her communion, and primarily and pre-eminently to her most powerful satellite and champion in Europe—France. Its fair realm became, under its deadly perversion, a charnel-house. The revocation of the Edict of Nantz, and Bartholomew's fatal day, had quenched in her bosom the religious reform, that might have enlightened and saved the philosophic reform; and had left that reform to run on, blind, wild, and godless. Italy, Austria, and Spain owed their apparent comparative exemption from the same disasters to the fact, that in those countries religious and philosophical reform, together with the reason and life of the nations, seemed smothered in one grave. The storm of philosophic revolution beat on England, but beat as beats the surf against her island. The comparative enlightenment of her masses, imperfect as it was, and the presence of well-armed and disciplined champions of her faith, which Protestant liberty had prepared, stood her instead in her hour of trial.

It was incidental also to a revolution in philosophy, such as we have above described, that in the application of the new method, before men had by trial learned the capacity of their instrument and the limits of its power, there should be developed new and partial systems of truth—parts of the great myriad-faced unity—but not yet combined in harmony. All partial systems, pursued in isolation and as the alone true, must produce distortion, absurdity, and ultimately, skepticism. Such was the case with the sensational and the ideal philosophies. Each represented a great truth; one the law of knowledge of the outer, the other that of the inner world; but either pursued exclusively and solitarily necessarily led to unbelief; one to materialism, the other to pantheism.

This evil tendency, incident to young and immature systems every where, manifests itself with especial frequency and mischief where the mind of nations is not armed in a measure against it by previous indoctrination in religious truth. Hence though both these schools abounded and one originated in England, they were comparatively innocuous till they passed to the Catholic realms of the Continent or countries where Protestantism abandoned its distinctive principle of spiritual liberty for—the despotism of its antagonist. It was only where liberty was unwonted, was seized violently, or its light broke in on blinded and imprisoned nations, that it wrought serious mischiefs.

Thus, looking at the philosophic revolution of the sixteenth and seventeenth centuries as effective of infidelity, we find the guilt of that efficiency resting, not with Protestantism, but the opposite ecclesiastic pole. That revolution was in itself a blessing. It was made otherwise only by a spiritual despotism, paralyzing and darkening the intellect and faith of nations, and making mental emancipation wild and mad from the sense of long enslavement and from the newness of liberty.

In conclusion we ask then, shall Protestantism, having emancipated the human mind from a thraldom that bound up all science, physical, metaphysical, political as well as theological, and having instaurated a philosophy of progress to which we owe all improvements, scientific and social, that divide us from ages of mediæval barbarism,—shall she have blame, because in so doing she rent away a subtle and adamantine scholasticism, with which Rome had bound the nations to her power; and because, in consequence, a false faith and a false philosophy perished together? And when nations thus emancipated, shall, because of the systematic darkening and repression of mind pursued by Rome towards them for ages, stagger and wander into strange and tortuous ways, at first, in the new light and liberty, shall Protestantism bear the sins of the despotism she attempted to overthrow? She found the world fast moored by the old philosophy—moored there for nearly two thousand years. She said, "Let us on upon our voyage." It was a great hour when she thus said "Let us go on;" she cut the hawsers, and, spite of wind and wave and current and storm, we have moved on and are still moving; we are fast leaving the rocks of the old coast—the shoals and quicksands and typhoons of unbelief that wait round those shores of death. We have already moved along hopefully and gloriously, through two centuries of the voyage of humanity; and, with God and Liberty to impel us, and an open Bible and free reason for our charts, we will go on unfearing.

I know there is a spiritual power in Christendom that abhors light and liberty; and rightly; it instinctively recognizes in them its mortal foes—which studiously aims to darken nations, and naturally; for darkness is the hiding of its power;—which anathematizes the free press and free speech and free schools, and reasonably; for it lives by the repression of the thought and utterance of mankind; within its pale ignorance is the mother of devotion—at whose borders the railroad and telegraph have been stopped as jealously as an invading plague; and with right discernment of its vital interests; for society can advance only over its ruins; with true instinct it quarantines literature and cordons itself, as it can, against ideas; for the spirit of the age would consume it with the breath of its mouth, and with the brightness of its coming. Naturally, therefore, *it* may look to the middle ages with regrets, as to its lost millenium; and regard the free movement given to the European mind in the sixteenth and seventeenth centuries, with sheer dismay and horror; not unnaturally it regards the philosophic revolution in these centuries, as the opening of the bottomless pit in the apocalypse, darkening the skies of Europe with its shapes and shades. But surely we, who believe in light and liberty, shall be slow to regard *them* as legitimately responsible for the denial of a God and religion of light and liberty. Is Protestantism to be condemned for the abuses and mischiefs incident to the emancipation of mind? Is liberty of thought and belief a curse? Bind a man in fetters and he will run off no precipice. Put out his eyes and he will never see false. Shall all men therefore be blinded and shut up in dungeons? Keep the car fast bound to the station house, and it will never run off the track. Is the conductor therefore that will not chain it up, responsible if it make a somerset down an embankment, or into a chasm, because of some neglected switch, or a drawbridge perversely or maliciously left open? No, give us eyes and hands, and steam-cars, and with all their risk, we thank you. So give society and give mind, liberty. *Let us move.* If we must perish, a hundred times better by the cataract than the cess-pool.

Protestantism, then, as a revolutionist of philosophy and emancipator of the intellect of Europe, were a mighty benefactor; even if chargeable with all the disasters to faith, and in consequence to society, exhibited in the eighteenth century. But she is not so chargeable. They were incidental, some of them, to a transition period in civilization; a step in philosophic reform, which was inevitable and necessary to social progress. Nay more, we affirm these evils were many of them so inseparable from that step, because of the abuses of that very church which now charges them on Protestantism as a crime; because of its abuse of the faith and worship of the world; its war on enlightenment and science, and the instinctive rights of the human soul. Protestantism is responsible so far as it apostatized from its first principle, *i. e.* so far forth as it ceased to be Protestantism, joined in the attempt at repression and enslavement of the human mind, and with the enemies of progress,

> "grew pale
> Lest men's judgments should become too bright,
> And their free thoughts be crimes, and earth
> Have too much light."

If Protestantism therefore be arraigned for its philosophy, as a crime, we are willing that Philosophy should step forward and plead her own cause. She may come before the court of History not merely with intrepidity; with *triumph* she may lift her hand to the great oath, that she has merited well of the race of man. She may say "I am the philosophy of liberty, life, progress. My defence—it is this great living world around you—this mighty present that bears you on. All that magnificent and infinite array of improvements in industrial arts, in mechanism, production and exchange; all these inventions and discoveries that arm man's hand with a grasp and sway of the forces of nature; all those advances in science, government, and in the general comfort and embellishment, the ennoblement and culture of life, that divide the seventeenth from the fifteenth century—these are my argument. I have brought society further in three hundred, than it traversed before in ten times three hundred years. I have spangled over zones with cities of machinery. I have made the desolate rock, and waste and dismal morass to bloom with purple and scarlet and gold. I have covered the seas with fleets that are borne by their own tempest against wind and wave and tide. I have stretched the loom of commerce in wares and ideas, between strange nations and across mysterious oceans. I have exalted the valleys and brought low the heights, have pierced the mountain, bridged vast and torrent rivers, and banded continents with iron roads. I have vastly increased and varied the productions of the earth, and the occupation and support of man. I have infinitely multiplied the manufacture and diffusion of appliances for the well-being of society; and have widened the intercourse of business and of thought among mankind. I mitigate disease. I disarm the plague. I draw off silently and innocuously the wrath of the thunder-cloud. I steal from light its pencil; I make the lightning the bearer of human thought, and the agent of a universal and simultaneous consciousness of nations. I have opened for man the hidden treasure-house of the mountains, the mysteries of the zones of eternal frost and fire, and the secrets of the seas and the skies; I have inaugurated him, as God decreed him at first, Lord of nature, and I have made him victor of storm and tide, of distance and solitude, of tropic heat and polar ice. In the spiritual and ideal realm also, I have placed man in the paths of an illimitable advance. I have imparted to him the key and method of the true Dialectic—the logic that shall grasp, analyze, and frame to new, glorious and mighty forms, the subtle and shifting phenomena of the world of thought. I have given the laws of perpetual progression in intellectual, moral and religious truth; and formularies that shall open to the soul new and wondrous fields of knowledge, ever widening, as far as is permitted the children of this life to gaze.

"Modern Civilization—with its legislation, economy and education, its institutions and improved methods and appliances for the elevation and enlightenment of the million—this is my mighty and glorious pupil; and I marshal it toward a future of indefinite grandeur, power and beauty. I have created and instaurated for society a science of itself, and am placing in its hands the directory of an endless march; ever onward and upward, till the philosophy of a new dispensation takes up its instruction on the plains of Heaven. My past achievements are but the promise of my infancy. I am yet but in the beginning of my ways. The boundless future is mine. I am the philosophy of life and growth; the genius and guardian of an infinite progress; and especially the elaborator, conservator and champion of genuine Faith. If I have been abused, so have all God's gifts—so has all liberty—so has light—so has life. Under these skies, death alone has no perversion, no insanity, no disease."

We will be content then, thus to leave the philosophy of Protestantism amid her own monuments to plead her own cause; confident that that plea is sufficient vindication of that communion that patronizes her.

The curse of the seventeenth and eighteenth centuries was not liberty or enlightenment. It was not that the sun had risen, but that an evil angel had poured out his vial of wrath on the orb of light; not able thereby to quench it, but giving it power to burn men as with fire. "And men were scorched with the great heat and blasphemed the God of Heaven."

CHAPTER IV.

MAMMONISM.

Rise of the Idea of Wealth to the Ascendency in European Society —Causes—Subsidence of Religious Passions—Old paths of National Aggrandizement closed up—Transfer of Ambition and Enterprise to new Desertions—Progress of Society in Wealth and Productive Art—The Era of Economies—Mississippi Schemes—East Indies—Ventures—South Sea Bubbles—The Money-God Supreme—The new Philosophy his Minister—Acme of his Reign at Paris under the Regent of Orleans—Law's Banking Scheme—The Saturnalia of Mammon—Rise of the Idea of Wealth a Necessity of Social Progress—Why so Disastrous to Faith?—Money-mania in France and England Compared– Dangers to Modern Society from Mammonism.

Another cause of the infidelity and irreligion of the eighteenth century, is found in *the new ideas that took possession of European politics and society* and in the consequent new direction given to national and individual life and effort. From the causes I have already noticed, the great religious passion and agonism of the sixteenth and seventeenth centuries had subsided. The religious idea was dethroned; and after the religious and political settlement of Europe by the treaty of Westphalia a new idea and passion rise to the ascendency in the European mind; namely those of WEALTH.

The great conflagration of the religious wars had burned out. Its fires had in a measure died away in the council chamber and the battle-field, and in the heart of nations. The hopes of decided ecclesiastical victory and of European empire, as between either of the great religious parties, had been perforce abandoned. The avenues to political aggrandizement through the alliance and aid of either of these parties, or by appeals to the religious passions which had animated them, had been closed up. The ambition of dynasties and the energies of nations, obstructed in these paths, henceforth seek another direction. By the law of transfer in the diseases of civilization, Mammonism takes possession of the European mind. The money-god sits supreme in all temples. Political economies are his gospels: and of these again, the new philosophy and the Encyclopædists are expositors.

Not that man had not always loved money; or that the lust of gold is the peculiar vice of any age. But in this era, it suddenly towers aloft. Supreme and almost alone in the cabinets and amid the peoples of Europe. It takes a precedence hitherto unexampled amid the ruling ideas of history and the passions of nations. We enter on the birth-era of mercantile, agricultural and manufactural systems, of navigation acts, colonial policies, of tariffs and trade-laws, of Mississippi Schemes, East India companies, South Sea Bubbles. Through maritime discovery and adventure, the direct commerce of the Indies newly opened, the gold and silver of Mexico and Peru, the progress of art, science and industry, and the general advancement of society, the wealth of nations was vastly increased and naturally became a ruling interest.

This new direction of the ruling ideas of Europe, in a measure necessitated by the obstruction of old paths of aggrandizement and the exhaustion or despair of religious passions, was moreover especially stimulated by the examples of England, Holland and Portugal. These were regarded as signal illustrations of the power of wealth to aggrandize nations; and as brilliant proofs of new paths to national greatness opened through commerce, manufactures, colonies, and political economies regulative of the industrial energies of peoples. Spain moreover was still dazzling Europe with her delusive spoils and trophies of colonial empire.

The treaty of Westphalia, adjusting and settling the limits of countries, left little room for territorial aggrandizement on the map of Europe; and the nations rushed with eagerness into the new game of greatness opened to them. They embark in schemes of national wealth, domestic and foreign. Through mercantile, manufactural, colonial and agricultural economies, Christendom is to become one vast plantation, manufactory, and exchange. Each county is to be husbanded as a garden. All art and industry —production, consumption, traffic—are to be perfectly systematized and mechanized; regulated as methodically as if one vast farm-house, workshop or mart. In short, nations are to become vast machines adjusted and worked for the production of wealth. Prussia, in its internal policy, becomes especially the model kingdom of this economic administration. Her territorial smallness was to be elaborated by economies to riches and greatness. Smith, Malthus and the economists are the evangelists of the New Era.

This direction of the mind of Europe was, like its emancipation in the realm of philosophy, probably a necessity of the stage of civilization which it had reached; a necessary means and consequence of the rise of the masses and the increased physical prosperity of nations. It was also—like the philosophic revolution synchronizing with it—productive of vast benefits and vast mischiefs to mankind. Vast industrial enterprises; improvements in the arts, appliances, comfort and power of human life; advancement in political and social institutions—in the police, security, production, the greatness and strength of nations—follow in its train. It stands related as cause and effect to the enfranchisement, enlightenment and elevation of the millions. As wealth and industrial and productive power rose in the social scale, the industrial and productive masses of course rose also. But together with those benefits this supremacy of the idea of wealth undoubtedly conspired powerfully with other causes to push the world from the realm of faith.

Mammonism, or the passion of wealth, is often charged as the *vice of Protestantism;* and with a color of truth; as a passion of wealth naturally associates itself with the successful pursuit of it; with the intelligence, activity, and enterprise which are produced and quickened by freedom, intellectual and civil, and which ensure success to such pursuits. Protestantism is undoubtedly a powerful stimulant to the mind of nations; it gives civilization a vastly increased power of every kind. Now wealth and power are wont to breed a passion for themselves. And this passion, not restrained by a vital Christianity, may become a sordid avarice, or rapacious ambition. Still we deem it no condemnation of a faith, that it brings wealth and power; especially as we have ample evidence in the history of modern Europe, that a church may impoverish nations without protecting their piety or virtue. No faith can shut out the *danger* of Mammonism, which does not shut out the faculty of wealth and sink a people toward a state of savageism. But the epidemic Mammonism of the seventeenth and eighteenth centuries was confined to the limits of no communion. Indeed the acme of its fever was in a country and capital of the Romish Faith.

But however caused and wherever it prevailed, it must unquestionably be noted as one of the most effective causes of the general skepticism of the age.

In the first place it is evident that the *supremacy of the passion of wealth* over civilization tends to *secularize* and *unspiritualize* it—to make it worldly and sensual. The declaration of our Saviour "ye cannot serve God and Mammon," holds ever true. If men cleave to the one, they will despise the other. If Mammon is enthroned, the face of Jehovah fades from the sky. The lust of gain, as a supreme principle of action and pursuit, degrades and corrupts the soul of the individual or the age. It is the most unheroic of passions. Magnanimity, sincerity, and generous sentiment, it wars on. Cunning, adroitness, finesse, are its virtues. Fraud, treachery, simulation, cold selfishness, are its means and ministers. It breeds a distrust of truth and heroism. Of course it is most widely at variance with the genius of Christianity, and little attracted to accept it. Most difficult is it for it, of all passions, to "enter into the kingdom of Heaven." It breeds moreover passions and vices which naturally seek to hide from God behind the veil of skepticism. It soon leaves little power of faith in anything noble and good, much less in God. There is terrible interaction between avarice and infidelity, as between corruption and death: one breeds the other.

Moreover the ascendency of this idea over society naturally associates with itself a *luxury* which emasculates and debauches the soul, and leaves it hardly energy or manhood for earnest Christian belief.

Thus the supremacy of the idea of wealth divides society more and more widely from religious faith. Long ascendant, it relaxes, enfeebles, corrupts, intoxicates it; till ultimately it goes into utter dissolution. This was illustrated in the course of civilization in the eighteenth century from the various causes enumerated. The lust of gold had rusted and corroded through the entire society of the times. The mightier and nobler false gods had disappeared from their shrines. Mammon, the "meanest and least erect of spirits that fell from Heaven," alone remained. The generous fever of the previous era had subsided. The pulse of humanity beat low; a slow cold corrupting palsy was icing stealthily around the heart and brain. Not now for God or glory or for beauty, but for gain were all things. For this men fought and plotted and chaffered; for this they made treaties, alliances, peace and war; for this they legislated, planted colonies, established manufactures, tariffs, trade-laws, colonial and commercial systems, coerced agriculture, instituted banks, inflated and exploded financial bubbles. For this they explored new seas and savage continents; they ravaged ancient realms; plundered barbaric monarchies; they dismembered kingdoms; they blotted old nationalities from the map of Europe; they prostrated the public law and political system of Europe in the dust. Everything revolved around the money question. Negotiation, legislation, foreign and internal policies, fulfillment or violation of treaties, manners, sentiment, opinions, literature, morality, and even religion, seemed grouped waiting around the question, will it pay? All things had their *money-representative* and equivalent. Faith, honor, heroism, patriotism, justice, chastity, piety—all had their prices. Power, empire, beauty, fame, grace, the favor of man, and even of God, were exposed for sale. Courts, monarchs, hierarchs, pontiffs, the church, and even Heaven itself in priestly finance, were venal. Genius, wit, taste, imagination, eloquence and song, philosophy and statesmanship, ministered, liveried and lacquered, in the antechamber of Mammon. Finance was god of the world, from hovel to palace, possessing each interest. In his train waited frauds, treacheries, disloyalties, hypocrisies; rapacity joined with waste, luxury with cruelty, pleasure mottled with murder, and "lust hard by hate." It was the reign of the money god who had taken possession of the vacant temple of European worship and the nations were prostrate before him.

"On a blazing throne of gems and gold,
The prize of many a damned soul,
There sat a king deformed and old,
Yellow and shrunk and foul:
The glittering bribe, the tempting purse
Spread there their unresisted lure,
For baits to prove the proud man's curse,
And keep the miser poor.
In his palsied hand the monarch gave
The radiant stone and blushing ore,
To mighty prince, and grovelling slave,
That knelt his throne before;
Gorging their food like worms i' the grave
And screaming loud for more.

"As amongst that cursed and greedy crew
The murderer thrust his blood-stained hands,
Where Beauty's palms of lily hue
The price of guilt demands:

Sin caught the despot in her arms,
And kissed his slimy jaws,
And shame exposed her wanton charms,
To gain his prized applause:
There the *hero* brought his hireling steel,
The bard his venal song,
While *patriots* sold the public weal,
The tyrants cherished wrong;
Monks uttered blasphemies to kneel
The favored of that throng.

"And they all devoured this precious food
With more than human zest,
Though bringing poison to the blood
And anguish to the breast:
Like vultures upon carrion fare,
They greedily fed on;
And fiercely seized their neighbor's share
Whene'er their own was gone:
As that crowned ghoul his gifts bestowed
With regal pomp and pride;
From those foul lips no language flowed,
But still the dupes he eyed,
Hurrying on to death's abode,
And cursed them as they died;
Shouting, 'Hail, Oh first of the sons of Ammon!
Hail to the great god Mammon!'"

In such a world, where the lust of gold had succeeded to religious enthusiasm and fanaticism, we do not wonder that faith could not abide. Nor again can we wonder that rapacity, cut loose from the restraints of faith, should have gone forth to make society desolate of the common virtues, and tear down the pillars of social order; to fill the seas with rapine, plunder and slay states and tear to shreds the public law of the world. We do not wonder that provinces were estimated at the productive and taxable energies of the human machines in them, and were bargained and transferred like herds of cattle. We do not wonder at finding infidel monarchs, ecclesiastics and philosophers uniting in their conspiracy against religion and law, now fraternizing in the revel of impiety, now plotting each other's robbery—as in case of the conspiracies of regal scoundrels for the dismemberment of Austria, Bavaria and Prussia—now pointing a witticism at Jesus Christ, and now pouring their ruffian armies upon Poland; now crowned with chaplets in the flower-festivals of the goddess of Reason, singing ballads preluding the advent of the godless golden age; now mingling in the bloody orgies of revolution that seemed to have torn open the infernal abyss.

This money-mania seems, like almost all distemperatures in modern civilization, to have exhibited the *acme of its madness at Paris.* This took place early in the eighteenth century, under the excitement of Law's famous banking scheme, in the time of the Regent of Orleans—a scheme which dazzled and attracted all Europe with the enormousness of its powers, prizes and promises. The scheme was to pay off two thousand millions of the debt of Louis XIV. by a single splendid stroke of finance. The bank was to be shored up by the commerce of the East and West Indies, and that of empires that were to spring up in the vast and mysterious Eldorado of the Mississippi. The imaginations of men were astounded with the magnificent hopes opening to them. It was as if an Australia or California were opened right in the capital of European civilization. At the time of the sale of the shares in 1719, the scene as described by Louis Blanc, indicates that the force of the madness could no further go.

In his History of the Causes of the French Revolution (page 175) he thus narrates:—

"We would surpass the limits of our subject were we to follow all the details of so vast an operation. But the effect which it produced has a too direct connection with that transformation of manners and that displacement of strength, out of which the revolution was to spring, for us not to pause over it.

"The excitement caused by the sale of the shares was intense. Who has not heard of the Rue Quincampoix and its stormy renown? Impatience of gain, the hope of retrieving a ruined fortune quickly, a presumptuous desire to brave destiny, a need of forgetfulness and of excitement, the poignant uncertainties which the heart in its folly dreads and seeks, the torments of which it is greedy, were all found strongly raised and at play, within the space of a few feet. Thus, courtiers, churchmen, courtesans, members of parliament, monks, abbés, clerks, soldiers, adventurers from every part of Europe, hastened to the Rue Quincampoix, to be rolled in a heap and mingled together in a huge pell-mell. The inequality of ranks disappeared there before the equality of human weaknesses and passions. The pride of the great ones of the earth was publicly drawn out to receive an exemplary chastisement in the eyes of the multitude. Fraternity reigned through stock-jobbing until something better turned up. Prelates dragged the Roman purple through the mob,. and princes of the blood bought or sold the paper between courtesans and lackeys. Even foreign sovereigns had their representatives in the thickest of this crowd, which was by turns drunk with hope or frozen by alarm, a confused, entangled, palpitating crowd, which the ebb and flow of play agitated incessantly, and from which a sinister noise arose. There was not a house in the famous street which was not divided into dens for speculators. Avidity took up its abode in them from the roof to the cellar. They stock-gambled by the light of the sun, and also by that of torches. To own a miserable shop in this quarter, was to have one's hand upon a gold mine. * * * * There were offices for sale and purchase; here was that of the Sieur le Grand, the treasurer of France, there that of the Sieur Negret de Granville, an old farmer of the aids and domains. A place was wanted to write upon; they had recourse to living desks, and the unfortunate made fortunes by hiring out their shoulders; they would have hired their souls; as long as the fever lasted, paper had the advantage over gold which the imagination has over the reality. Thus two men drew their swords one day in the street, the seller of shares wishing to be paid in paper, and the buyer of them wishing to pay in gold. The confusion soon became so great, that it became necessary to have a guard of archers, commanded by an officer of the Short Robe, at each end of the street. Regular agitations still more terrible succeeded this tumultuous agitation. The Le Blancs, the Verzenobres, the Andrés, the Pavillons, the Fleurys, commanded the movements by their emissaries, and kept the key of the storm-bag. * * * * * There was a general upsetting of fortunes; there was a metamorphosis in situations, comparable only with the ancient Saturnalia. * * * * The Duke de Bourbon and the Prince de Conti, were at the head of the speculators of renown, and the nobles followed in crowds. Many of the gentry surrounded the door of Law, the chief distributor of subscriptions, and passed whole hours there waiting for Law's presence, with a sordid anxiety, begging a look from him as a favor, and wearying his contempt by the excess and degradation of their cupidity. Not content with flattering him, recently an obscure stranger, and the son of a goldsmith of Edinburgh, they flattered his mistress, his daughter, still a child, even Thierry his valet. The court of Law was increased by many women of quality, momentarily escaped from the court of the Regent, and the governor of the bank became the object of their pursuits, the ardor of gain silencing their shame. Nothing was omitted, which was of a nature to dissipate old prestiges. It was in the company of the Targez, and the Poterats, that Louis Henry de Bourbon, the Marshal d' Estrées, the Prince de Valmont, the Baron Breteuil, managed the business. In the list of the directors of the India Company, might be read by the side of the name of the Regent of France, that of Saint Edme, known at the fair of Saint Laurent as the chief of the mountebanks. * * * * * A great lord, the Marquis d'Oyse, the son and younger brother of the Duke de Villars-Brancas, was shameless enough to take the daughter of the stock-gambler Andre, only three years old, as his wife, on condition that her dowry should be paid in advance."

Surely in a world with such a central scene we need not wonder that infidelity coupled with Mammonism seemed to have poisoned the moral life of universal society.

We point therefore to the ascendency of the idea of wealth, in the cabinets of princes and in general society, as one of the causes of skepticism; yet not a cause, be it noted, *in itself alone necessitating such a result;* but powerfully and fatally coöperating with other causes in the production of it. In view however of its efficiencies towards a result so universal and so disastrous, we are compelled to inquire what gave this cause in this era such a peculiar malignancy? What made the pursuit of wealth in that age so godless and so corrupting?

The passion of wealth is one of the dominant passions of our own time. It leaps through the veins of our universal civilization like a burning fever; still I think I may say the age is not infidel. What then gave its peculiar virus of infidelity and godlessness at that time? There must have been elements especially malignant conspiring and blending with it.

There were causes inherent in the history of the times and in the stage of civilization which Europe had attained, giving increased prominence and power to wealth, and stirring to the pursuit of it, with the intensity of a new and strange passion. The very increase of wealth in itself and the general causes elevating the industrial masses and creative of a third estate, necessitated such a consequence. But nevertheless a step essential in the progress of civilization, and requisite to the development of its power and to the accomplishment of vast and benificent physical, and to social and even moral achievement; such a step in the life of society, as was that out of which the idea of wealth rose to power, we are confident, God would have enabled society to take, without consequences so dreadful, but for great crimes of society itself and a most guilty feebleness or neglect or apostasy of the great moral vitalizer of society—the Church, or the body representing Christianity.

The malignant, epidemic Mammonism of the age demands our attention both as effect and cause. As an effect, it undoubtedly points us in part to the very causes that we have before noticed in this discussion as *directly* producing infidelity. It was because the Church, over most of Europe despotic, and in many countries, and especially in that where this madness raged most fiercely, warring on human reason and enlightenment, had lost its grasp and control of the age—had no power to purify, moderate or direct aright its passions. The Church—the power representative of Christianity—by its denial of man's instinctive right of private judgment, and by its cruelties towards the assertor of those rights, and by associating itself with political tyranny through almost the entire continent, had brought on itself the hatred and scorn of mankind; and had consequently no power to perform for society, when tried by the passion of wealth, the proper function of a moral guardian and curator. It could not discharge the office of a religion, viz., to bind, curb, moderate and temper the desires and impulses of society when impelled to disastrous and guilty excess. Its oppression moreover had kept nations in perpetual moral pupilage, had dwarfed and crippled their moral energies, and impaired their power of independent self-government and self-restraint. Society consequently encountered the temptation without the habit or power of resistance, and it is not strange it was overborne. It must be so with any faith formed without the free exercise of the right of private judgment. It is not genuine faith. It is a mere sham. It has no foundation in our self-consciousness, none in perceived evidence. It has no logic to defend itself against its own doubts or the assaults of others. The consciousness of never having proved itself by personal examination, or the examination of others in whose opinion it reposes its trust, must carry a fatal timidity and feebleness into all its results. In the time of temptation such faith will fall away; and that, whether it be the faith of individuals or of nations. When it ceases to be a superstition or a fanaticism, it is nothing. It ever is and must be a most miserable defence against either irreligion or unbelief; or any of those passions that from time to time sweep society like moral storms. Add to this feebleness necessarily incidental to any faith under coercion and restriction of examination, the sense of wrongs inflicted tyrannously and cruelly on the private reason and the conscience; the indignation and scorn arising in the mind from the attempt fraudulently to palm off, or authoritatively to enforce, the most puerile falsehoods and absurdities, and the most drivelling superstitions. Add the disgust that must arise in it, at seeing a religion without morality, a Christianity without charity, a Church at once superstitious and sensual, fanatic and hypocritical, licentious and tyrannical; add all these and we shall see forces enough at work utterly to strip religion of its power over the epidemic lusts of nations or eras, be they for gold or empire, and to cause social distemperatures to be left to run their course in entire riot; enough to push the human mind from the regions of its twilight faith into the thick darkness of irreligion and infidelity; and to impel it on to that madness of worldly passion and pursuit that arises from dimness or despair of the future, and crushes our eternal aspirations into this hour of life.

In proof of the correctness of this reasoning, we appeal to the comparative experience of the different countries of Europe which passed through the trial of the money-epidemic together. Where did the money madness strike deepest, and leave the most deplorable consequences? In Protestant or Catholic Europe? In Catholic. The storm of trial beat hard upon England—harder than perhaps on any other nation in Europe, in proportion as her industrial energies were most active and most stimulated by civil liberty, and upon her, gushed most profusely the golden stream of wealth. But though the national mind may have reeled a moment, it was not intoxicated nor overborne. The snaring influences of a world's commerce, and almost a world's wealth, of a national policy eminently mercantile, of interests and institutions, and foreign and domestic administration swayed by finance—all these were around the English mind. But there was in that mind, imperfect as was English Protestantism, enough of the energy of Christian truth and liberty to withstand these influences. That mind, as far as the great mass of the nation were concerned, held fast its sobriety and its loyalty to Christianity, and almost stood alone erect in Christendom. In France, on the other hand —the head of Catholic Europe—the excesses of atheism and of the money phrenzy were both wildest and nearly synchronous. Why was this? Absolute power in Church and State had made minds in her, inert and paralytic, or insurgent and disloyal toward Christianity, and exposed her defenceless to the corruptions of Mammon.

In the other country some degree—though imperfect—of spiritual liberty, had educated and disciplined the mind of the nation to self-sustained and energetic faith; to love Christ and Christianity independent of the Church, and armed it with deep and steadfast vital principles. Spain and other Catholic powers, that were less affected by the prevalent passion and enterprise for wealth, and which were not swayed so disastrously by it to infidelity, owed their partial exemption simply to the fact that despotism, civil and spiritual, had there done its deadly work with a more hideous completeness—had through the terrible energy and thoroughness of the Inquisition, so utterly quenched spiritual liberty and enlightenment, that the nation sank below the circle of the ideas of the age, and was in a great measure cut off from modern civilization. They escaped the perils of the transition period because they were stationary. They had no emancipation of mind, no revolution of philosophy, no rise of a third estate; they were exempt from the perils of progress and corruptions of enterprise. They escaped convulsion in permanent paralysis; the dangers of youth, in the imbecility of perpetual childhood. They fell below the range of the temptations and dangers of the period. To the degree that they were less afflicted by defiant and frantic atheism, they owed their exemption to a slavish superstition and abject ignorance. They had not life enough for fever, or spasm, or delirium. The same oppression that had suppressed Protestantism in them, had nearly crushed the vitality out of their civilization, and they had less of throes and agony only because they were nearer death.

The difference of the effects of despotic repression on minds, as between France and Spain, was the difference between killing a man and putting his eyes out. In one, the national mind seemed utterly crushed and smothered; in the other, it was blinded as it regards religion, but the passions of life and fever of intoxication were rioting as fiercely in the veins as ever. In France despotic repression had driven thought into wide and wild paths every way; but had shut up avenues to the true faith. In Spain it seemed to have quenched thought itself.

To the common charge, therefore, that Mammonism or the undue ascendency of the idea of wealth in communities—is a vice of Protestantism, we answer: it is obnoxious to this imputation only as it produces that industrial activity, skill and energy, and that prosperity and enlightenment of the masses, and that financial accumulation, enterprise and policy, from which the ascendency of this passion may spring. It makes nations money-loving, simply as it makes them money-getting and money-having. There is a faith that usually enforces its voice of poverty on nations if not on its acolytes and devotees—which delivers from Mammonism, by removing its prizes, by destroying the industrial energies, intelligence, art, enterprise; which wait on freedom of thought, and which alone enable nations successfully to enter into the competitions of production and traffic.

But alas, we find that nations can be poor without being pure; that idleness, ignorance, thriftlessness and mendicity are no guaranty of Christian faith and virtue. We find, again, where the despotism over thought has not succeeded in extinguishing fiscal enterprise and prosperity, it leaves the passion generated of and proper to that enterprise and prosperity, the most wild, exorbitant and without moral curb. It was, we may notice, in a country not Protestant that the money-mania was maddest and deadliest to the faith of nations.

This chapter in the history of the past admonishes not of the safety or desirableness of poverty, but of the necessity of counteracting the dangers which an era of Mammonism, like the one in which we live, must ever bring to faith and life, by the protective and restorative power of a free, vigorous and enlightened Christianity.

The theme is one of profound and solemn relevancy to our times. The melancholy cataclasm of the last century warns us of present peril. The lust of gold leaps through all the veins of the modern world. It burns through all our civilization. All passions and pursuits converge in this. All the prizes of society are in the gift of Mammon. The multitudinous, multifarious, infinite business of the world—its productions, manufactures, exchange—all are a constant discipline to the love of money. If another era of unbelief awaits us, we shall enter it through the portals of Mammon. The path to that abyss will be draped with purple and shine with gold. Railways, steamships, mysteries of mechanism, the wonders of art, Californias, Australias, will marshal us that way. The spirit of the age already feels the spell of the mighty fascination. From this one thing only shall save us. No glittering cathedral, or purple hierarchies, or pomp of superstition, or awe of antiquity or authorities; no slavish, no dogmatic, no ignorant, no dead faith, nothing but the energy, the power, the intelligence, the spirit, the life of an earnest, enlightened faith, communing freely with the Scriptures and the Spirit of Truth.

Never in any age has there been such vital need of an earnest, active, intelligent and free Church, as now and in our own country. The richer our prosperity, the more intense our necessity. Without it the golden stream on which we sail, bears us surely to the doom of ancient Tyre and the nations of old—whom riches slew. We hurry through Mammonism to godlessness and dissolution. From the era when Jugurtha departing from Rome, shook vengefully his hand just threatened with Roman chains, at that capital of the earth, with the ominous menace, "Ah doomed city! sold, if only you can find a purchaser;"—from that era, her faith and her manhood sickened together under the blight of the lust of gold. No longer glory or country or religion; no temple or shrine or home; but gain, plunder, luxury—these were the battle-cry, that led on her legions. The overspreading Mammonism and Epicurism, together with the Atheism, that followed, are abundantly noted in the orators and satirists and historians of the close of the Republic and the beginning of the Empire. So along that future of infinite wealth, and infinite stimulants to the passions for wealth, opening to our age, this generation will walk with more peril than through a field bristling with the arms of a world. A faith that walks with a living Christ and an open Bible, that is active, manly, enterprising, beneficent and free, and which commands the intellect and conscience of the age, alone can save us. Without this the golden clouds that float over and about us, will settle down all around our sky, and we shall see beyond no God, no Heaven, no immortality, nor the frightful grave that waits us, hid in that "field of the cloth of gold."

CHAPTER V.

SPIRITUAL DESPOTISM.

Spiritual Despotism, the Cause of Causes—Era of Absolutism—Double Despotism over Europe — Treaty of Westphalia — Military Monarchies—Hopelessness and helplessness of the Millions—Intellectual repression—Mind driven from the Practical to the Speculative—License of Speculative Thought—The World Undermined—War on Private Judgment—A War on the Faith of Nations—The Spiritual Power Darkened and Emasculated—Intellectual imbecillity of the Church—Ecclesiastical Literature in Protestant and Catholic Europe.

THE theme we now propose to consider is SPIRITUAL DESPOTISM, related as a cause to the *Great Apostasy of Christendom* in the eighteenth century. We wish to direct especial attention to *it*, not simply because of the importance of it as a *fact*, in its historic relations to the particular phenomenon we investigate, but because of its essential and immortal malignancy as a *principle*, in all times and all forms, and because, like a chronic cleaving curse, it fastens on society through all changes. Hideously prominent, it stands out on the page of both logic and history, as the enemy of faith, and in countless subtle, shifting disguises, it walks the whole earth, this hour. It lingers in every clime; in every civilization; in every communion; perhaps I might say without paradox, in every human bosom. It is a spirit of that sort that cometh not out without prayer and fasting, and seldom too without tearing the victim it leaves.

The great disaster to faith, of modern society in the transition era of its philosophy and civilization in the seventeenth and eighteenth centuries, is often charged on the principle of *Liberty* or *Protestantism*. But history as well as philosophy, seem to us unmistakably to point to directly the opposite principle—*Despotism*, as the great cause of the defection of the human mind from religious faith during the above period. She points especially to the *double* despotism of Church and State, that peculiarly marks this period. In baleful *conjunction*, civil and ecclesiastical tyrannies hung in *double orb* over the sky of Europe for a century; like the plague-struck sun in the apocalypse, tormenting the nations.

By despotism, I mean lordship, mastery, dominion, of man over man, or mind over mind; the forceful rule of the opinion, reason, or will, of the one, as matter of authority and command, over those of the many. Such lordship applied to religion, we call spiritual despotism; to politics, political despotism; to philosophy and science, intellectual despotism.

Spiritual despotism wielded by the Church, is named ecclesiastical. Ecclesiastical despotism united with the State, as ally, instrument or master, is termed politico-ecclesiastical despotism. By spiritual despotism in this chapter, I mean either despotism wielded by the spiritual power, or that over spiritual interests.

In the seventeenth and eighteenth centuries, the human mind was peculiarly feeling the curse of a double or rather triple despotism; which had been plaguing the earth for ages, but then with especial and combined pressure, crushed down humanity. Intellectual, spiritual, political—all united, and with peculiar virulence, in its triple hideousness, presented a terrible completeness of tyranny, almost without parallel in the worst ages. It seemed like an attempt to smother the life of the world. Attempt, I say; for happily the triumph, the absolutism of this tyranny, was never an achieved fact. Its attempt had in God's mercy been deferred in human history, till it could be only an attempt. The movement was too late for perfect success. Nevertheless it wrought in the earth a mighty curse. It was the *repression* and *perturbation* caused by the attempt of this triple despotism to master society, that drove the mind of Europe wide and wild from its healthful and natural course. It was not the *emancipation* of the reason, but the attempt to *fetter* it when partially emancipated, that wrought the mischief. It was not the stream itself, but the dykes and dams thrown across its otherwise beneficent and fertilizing current, that caused the inundation that swept the world.

The seventeenth and eighteenth centuries were peculiarly the era of absolute monarchy in Europe. The period of which we treat (1648—1790), opens with the scene of *thrones surrounded with standing armies.* The *military* has succeeded to the *feudal monarchy.* The terrible convulsion of one hundred and fifty years of religious war has torn feudalism to pieces, or has broken, impoverished and prostrated it, all through Western Europe. The new finance of nations, now feeds armies formerly sustained by feudal loyalty and treasure; indeed, far vaster standing forces than feudal history ever knew. Thus the new-born political economy and the science of wealth marking the progress of society in various interests, become the arts of tyranny. The invention of gunpowder, and the new arts and appliances of war, have converted it into a science of mere mechanized masses; a mathematical problem, rather than a game of chivalry.

Christendom has just emerged from the great drawn battle of the Reformation; but has emerged *in armor.* It now presents an array of states in a permanent armed *truce.* Large military establishments, created by ages of religious warfare and sustained by the new finance, are now deemed necessary by states to *watch* and *guard against each other*, in time of peace. The throne appears no longer girt with baronial swords, but surrounded by myriads of bayonets; not only as a defence against aggression from abroad, but as a ready and terrible instrument of enforcing a mechanic obedience at home; and of repressing and crushing the liberties of the subject millions.

And, to make the despotism more oppressive, those liberties have now no constitutional or institutional defences. The restrictions of feudalism, the rights of estates, the privileges of classes and orders, baronial prerogatives and provincial liberties, had to a great extent perished in the convulsions of the previous period. There was now no breakwater against the central despotism or monarchy. Nations are seen prostrated with no intervention of shield or defence before the throne.

Under the tyranny of Charles the Fifth, and still more under the Tiberian despotism of Philip Second the feudal and provincial liberties of Spain, order by order, province by province, and kingdom by kingdom, had been beaten down. The dark bigotry of

Ferdinand Second, had, after generations of cruel and religious wars, effected the same in the vast estates of Austria—Hungary, Bohemia and Austria proper; and at the close of thirty years war, in consequence of the long rule of violence and mere arms, Germany, throughout its multitude of states, presents a group of petty or powerful military despotisms; while Prussia, under the ambition of the House of Brandenburgh, exhibits itself, in this as in other respects, one of the most perfect types of the tendencies of the age. In France, the aristocracy has for the most part perished in the *civil wars;* and baronial parliamentary liberties lie crushed beneath the throne of the Bourbons. In Sweden, Denmark, and the Northern powers, the same tendency toward absolute monarchy is manifested. In England, it is the rule of the Tudors and the Stuarts. In short, as I said before, it is the era of absolutism; the baron has sunk in the courtier: the privileges of estates are prostrate; and royalty stands alone amid its cordon of mechanic and mercenary legions; alone, save that in the evil alliance with it, appears the spiritual power. To this, I especially wish to call attention, this junction of despotism, all through Europe, during the seventeenth and eighteenth centuries, as a portentous feature of the times. State is everywhere the guardian of faith. Lord, ally, or servant of the

Church. This is true both of Protestant and Catholic Europe. The Church, whether national or papal, is in either case despotic, and the abettor and confederate of absolute power in the State. It is the instrument and accomplice of the throne, in a conspiracy against the liberties of mankind; leaving no longer hope in the separation and division of tyrannies.

I have said this was true in Protestant States, as well as Catholic. In this, it is true, the Protestant Church (so called) is in conflict with its vital principles; but it becomes none the less, to the extent of its despotic practice, equally responsible for the disastrous consequences to faith, arising from the forceful repression or perturbation of the European mind, and from placing Christianity in seeming antagonism to liberty and progress.

It is spiritual despotism in alliance with civil, that I wish to point at, as one great cause of the defection of Christendom from Christianity in the eighteenth century; and that, whether in Protestant or Catholic States. And if the mischiefs were less universal or permanent in the former, than in the latter, it was because despotic Protestantism was a solecism and inconsistency in itself; convulsed, rent and made powerless often by its own antagonisms. Its life-principles ever warred on its despotic practice, broke the edge of its despotism while it survived, and were destined finally to destroy it.

The Treaty of Westphalia made no provision for the spiritual liberty of individuals. In that great settlement of Europe in 1648, there is no recognition of the right of private judgment. Protestantism becomes a *religio licita*, a legitimated religion, in the European family of States; that is all. The religious independency of nations, as between themselves, is guaranteed. But this independency was in effect only the equal religious absolutism of potentates; an equal license to crush down dissent in their own realms, undisturbed by their neighbors. No guard is taken for the spiritual liberties of the subject. The millions were handed over to their rulers, with slight exceptions, as mere dumb driven cattle; to be coerced by pains and penalties, at pleasure, into conformity with the creed and order of their despots.

Thus everywhere the despotic State, by natural affinities, draws to itself the despotic Church. Secular and spiritual tyrannies coalesce and conspire; and they wield in execution of their mandate, vast machine-like masses of military force; such as Europe has never seen before, since the Roman Empire.

To this baleful alliance and double pressure of despotisms in the seventeenth century, made more stifling still with the weight of a ponderous military arm, is to a great extent attributable the religious eclipse during the century that follows.

This result accrued in various ways. In the first place, this double despotism turns the mind of the world out of its regular and healthful course. To the obstruction and repression of the human mind in its ordinary and practical direction, in the seventeenth century, must be ascribed much of its wild, erratic, revolutionary, often destructive, career in the ages following. The despotisms, political and ecclesiastical, that towered above nations, forbade all action, all speech, all question, and as far as possible, all thought, implicating themselves. And as this covered both worlds, what was left? They ordained themselves sacred, inviolate, forbidden themes. The human mind might not look that way with question. Around the throne and the altar, it was to prostrate itself, blind, and in silence. Of its great, immediate, palpable, wrongs and rights, of the tyrannic organisms of society meeting it everywhere, of ecclesiastical or political institutions, of laws, parliaments, estates, church liberties and reforms, church creeds and rituals—of themes like these, it might not breathe a free whisper; at least, all speech and literature must keep so far aloof from the actual world, as to avoid the jealous suspicions and espionage of the spiritual and secular tyrants of that world. All thinking must pass the censorship of pope, prelate, monarch and premier. Theology and politics became in consequence, to a great extent, shut against the human mind. The ideal and speculative was the only field left open to it. Into that it plunged: the infinite abstract became its realm and its laboratory.

Hence the wide severance soon exhibited between the speculative and practical. Men took their revenge for the tyrannous restrictions thus enforced on thought and speech within, by giving themselves unbounded license beyond those restrictions. There was none of the moderation and sobriety ever impressed on thought, by bringing its conclusions to the test of experiment, and into relation to the actual world. Men plunged into wild and daring, fantastic and impious vagaries of philosophy, utterly careless because they were all mere speculative vagaries, nothing more: it was all heat lightning; or at least, thunder in mid-sky. Nobody could be hit; it never touched the common earth or existent actual interests, and never was to do so. Thus mind entered with reckless freedom into the realms of abstract thought; none of the common healthful restrictions of actuality or practicality limiting it. Literature became in consequence conjectural, ideal, empirical, all-questioning, all-daring. Free thought left the common earth to plunge into the dark deeps below, or to soar into the mist and vapor above; till society was all undermined beneath, and its sky was veiled all over with subtle and fantastic cloud-work, ready to turn to masses of storm on coming generations. *This was the first great mischief of those despotisms*—this *forcing the human mind away from its course;* driving it from affairs themselves which might have moderated and regulated it, to the abstract principle which lay at the basis of affairs, and with which, because they were abstract, it was tempted to deal with the wildest and most capricious license.

It is astonishing to observe, in the middle of the eighteenth century, the portentous chasm which was thus made to yawn between the speculative and the actual world—a chasm it was to take the ruins of European civilization, the wreck of its oldest monarchies, and the corpses of ten millions of men to fill up. Yet men were never more unconscious of the precipice to which society was brought. They seemed to have had no idea that the speculative might ever attempt to become the practical; the ideal, the real. Courtiers and monarchs, in Versailles and Potsdam and Vienna, mouthed of Cato and

Harmodius and names of classic freedom and regicide heroism; even Frederick the Great, so called, the most absolute and not least sagacious of the tyrants or his time, could talk loftily of Brutus and the king-killers, and vapor in heroic platitudes of democratic liberties and magnanimities; little thinking the earth could still breed democrats and assassins of kings. The infidel epigram flashed and hissed amid the brilliant circles of Paris and Berlin and Petersburgh, with utter thoughtlessness that those glittering sparkles were setting the world on fire—were igniting a magazine below altar and throne and universal society. Speculations on the social contract were as carelessly embraced, and caricatures of royal or hierarchical vice and folly, were as heartily and as recklessly laughed at, as if they were theories and picturings of the man in the moon. I need not argue that such a state of the public mind was favorable to skepticism—it *was* skepticism; striking through all the foundations of the actual world; yet in the deeps, but soon to emerge to the surface of affairs.

Now when we reflect on the mighty startle and impulse given to the human mind by the achievements in science, art and discovery, and by the conflict of religious ideas, in the seventeenth and eighteenth centuries; and that the world was just emerging from the era of Luther and Calvin and Zuingle, of Copernicus and Columbus, and the inventor of Strasburgh who wrought mightier than they all; when we reflect that it was in such an age that such an arrest was attempted of the human mind, we shall not wonder at the terrible energy with which that mind was impelled into new and wild ways; nor that driven from ecclesiastical and political reform, it should with terrible force address itself to a revolution in the realm of philosophy—to the questioning of first principles and to the destruction and reconstruction of the foundations of all belief. In short, across the current of the world's mind, thus dashing down the rapids of the previous age, civil and spiritual despotism threw their massive and gloomy structures. No wonder they caused an overflow that flooded the whole earth; and that the violence of the waters made them insinuate through the deeps below, and fret against the foundation of those structures, till they were all undermined, and tottering over a hideous abyss.

This crushing repression was attempted on the minds of Europe in all the eagerness and enthusiasm of new light and liberty, and under the intensest stimulant of novel and startling ideas and discoveries. Christendom had never known such an era; the world seemed as a seething, molten world, in genetic agitation. It was such a world, that was at once overlaid by vast strata of adamantine despotisms. No wonder the earthquake was bred in the deeps and soon burst forth; that those strata were torn asunder, and the infernal world seemed to yawn under modern civilization.

But again, while this terrible despotism over the society of Europe in the seventeenth and eighteenth centuries, was producing an impulse toward a profound and universal skepticism in the realm of philosophy, tending to propagate itself through all thought and feeling, it was especially effectual to generate unbelief in the realm of religion. It necessitated this first by *its war on the right of private judgment* in matters of religion. Despotism seated on the pontifical or on the royal and archiepiscopal thrones of Europe, with steel-clad legions as its instrument, forbade the nations below to reason or judge for themselves, on questions of religious faith. The exercise of this right they pursued as high treason against God and the king. They pronounced it liable to the extremest punishment of human power and the pains of eternal damnation. Each State assumed to be responsible for the religious belief of its subjects; and almost every State in Europe, Protestant or Catholic, in the seventeenth century, established platforms of faith and worship for its subjects, which it was bound to enforce at all hazards. To wink at dissent, was a crime against Heaven and the souls of men. Princes also were impelled the more strongly towards the enforcement of religious uniformity, from the spectacle of the religious and civil wars of the previous age of the Lutheran reform; a spectacle leading them to regard religious uniformity as essential to national unity and strength. Everywhere they had seen, in that intolerant period, theological dissensions fomented and exasperated to civil wars.

From these and other causes, all over Christendom, at this period, the potentates and prelates of Europe present the nations with creeds; to deny which was to bring on them the secular as well as spiritual sword; even to doubt which, exposed to the pains of hell. In short they denied to individual man the right of reasoning at all on what they had once determined in spiritualities. The command to him was simply, "Believe; and believe as his masters told him; and as often as they told him; and as fast as they told him." Indeed sometimes, as under Henry VIII. of England, it was hard for the subject to keep up with the swift-footed changing faith of his tyrant. He might be burned for believing to day what he would have been hung for denying yesterday, and what he might be shot for doubting to-morrow. Belief was regarded as being as facile and reasonable an object of command, as paying a tax, or putting on a uniform.

Such was the theory and practice of governments towards religion, nearly all over Europe. But is it not evident that such treatment as this of the human mind, necessitates skepticism, as it regards the matter whereon it is so treated? that to attempt to guard any article of belief by a despotism over thought, must of necessity bring that article into doubt? You compel the very distrust you would smother! Instead of securing uniformity of belief by suppressing private judgment, it is clear, both in the light of fact and philosophy, you make true belief impossible. In the first place, as far as you can repress private judgment, you take away the power of all belief. Talk and argue as you please against the right of private judgment, it is palpable, it is only through its exercise you can believe anything. You may as well require me to see without my own eyes, or hear without my own ears, as to believe without my own private judgment.

Dogmatic belief is no exception to this statement. You believe on authority. You must first sit in judgment upon that very authority. Even in case of a doctrine, received on the authority of the Scripture, our private judgment must first admit that authority, from examination of its authenticity, genuineness and inspiration. The mind must exercise its freedom in renouncing its freedom. It must *use* its right of private judgment, to decide it has no right of private judgment. To speak of belief then without private judgment, is clearly absurd in the nature of things. As it has been well said by Morell (532d page): "In matter of fact, private judgment must be exercised whether we will or not. We come into God's world without any mark upon our spirits to tell us where we are to find the truth; and it is equally a matter of private opinion, whether we determine to work out our own systems of religious belief for ourselves, or whether we determine to yield to the authority of others. In short, if the validity of reason be once destroyed, nothing, not even revelation (which must be received through its medium) can save from universal skepticism."

It is evident then, a war on the right of private judgment, is a war on all belief. As far as it is successful, it must beget universal skepticism. The more stringent and omnipresent the despotism, the more terrible the destruction of genuine belief among nations. Force may extort verbal profession, and coerce a nominal uniformity; genuine, real belief, it can no more produce than force can make a proposition in geometry true or false, or alter the science of optics. The submission of millions, or their nominal assent, under the terror of force, cannot prove a single truth, or make a single believer, throughout all generations. Belief has its own laws and conditions, as much as electricity; its necessary precedent, law and condition, is that of perceived evidence; it is impossible it should come without this. Force has nothing at all to do with it. It is utterly and eternally alien from it: not by the breadth of worlds, but by the difference of nature and being; it is of another universe. Force may produce hypocrisy, or a sham and semblant faith, and these by the loathing reaction they provoke, and by the general distrust they breed, become a prolific source of skepticism; both in the individual conscious of the falsehood, and in observers. This has ever been one of the curses of a hollow faith, and of a tyrannous church. They discredit all genuine belief; and smite the earth with the plague of universal distrust.

In the second place, war on the right of private judgment enfeebles belief, where it does not destroy it. Belief will be impotent or will have the mastery of the soul, just in proportion as the mind is conscious of having in some form used its own private judgment, *i. e.* its own reason, in the matter. Hence tempted restriction on this right afflicts nations with feebleness or paralysis of faith; which thus becomes inadequate to resist any strong or subtle attacks, and is ever ready in the hour of trial to pass to doubt or a negation of all belief. Such faith is faith without courage or armor, yea, faith without substance at all; a mere shadowy, empty form.

Thus spiritual despotism, when the pressure of fear is removed, is ever the prolific parent of infidelity. And thus, in the ages of which we speak, it is evident, independent of the subsequent melancholy testimony of history, that despotism must have prepared a general era of unbelief, by making, when completely successful, genuine faith impossible; and by rendering, when it was partially so, all belief timid, distrustful, feeble, and incapable of resistance to the epidemic temptations and passions of the age. Indeed, I am sure I need not argue this point here. Deny to us the right of private judgment, and we have no judgment at all; mere negation, no belief, no faith, are all that is left us.

I cannot sufficiently express my detestation of a doctrine that thus strips man of humanity. Renounce my right of private judgment and that in matters of religion! What is it but to renounce my intellectual personality!—my moral manhood!—my very spiritual identity!—to abdicate the prime prerogative of my eternal soul! Such a war as we have described, waged by spiritual despotism on this right, could only darken nations; leave them to grope on their gloomy way without knowledge or manhood; and with no principles to withstand the sophisms of the caviller, or to rebuild their religious belief when superstitions and falsities had been rent away. Just as in historic fact, the nations of central Europe *were* left, when, under the attacks of the new and daring skeptical philosophy, the faith of kingdoms seemed almost to fail at once. This is the second great mischief of despotism. For fear of obliquity of vision it puts the world's eyes out. In stifling reason it smothers belief. Thus despots that exulted in thinking to exterminate heresies with the sword, found soon they had been striking at faith itself. Thinking to extirpate a cancer, they had stabbed the heart of religion itself, and lo! as in a moment, it seemed to go down to the grave.

But sad as are the above consequences of religious tyranny on the faith of *nations*, its first and deadliest mischiefs are inflicted on the *Spiritual Power itself*—the Church; which is both its instrument and its victim. Let us then, in tracing the consequences of despotism in the seventeenth and eighteenth centuries, look first at its effects here. We shall find it, whichever way we look, a Devil whose name is Legion.

And first, such despotism as above delineated,

must emasculate and disarm the natural champions of religious faith among a people. It must breed in a church a logical imbecility and cowardice, an illiterateness and indolence, that shall make it incompetent to defend Christianity against its assailants; and when the enemy shall come in like a flood, there shall be none to lift up a banner against him. Thus it will produce infidelity, through intellectual imbecility in the spiritual order. Despotism effects this imbecility variously. First.—Its war on private judgment necessarily makes the faith of the spiritual order itself, as well as that of nations, feeble, ignorant and timid, as shown above. Second.—It takes away from churchmen the necessity of, and incentives to, intellectual culture and discipline, and induces a haughty indolence and arrogant security.—"What is the use or demand for argument and erudition, when simple authority and mere force can settle everything so much more summarily and unanswerably? Why vex my brains and disturb a luxurious ease to discover and arrange historical, philological or philosophical evidence to confute the misbeliever, when a brief *dash* of the pen to the magistrate or the official of the Holy Office, answers every purpose just as well? Yea, may be the more effectual to the saving of his soul, by bringing him more promptly to a sense of the evil of his ways. Certainly it is easier to imprison a man than to answer his arguments;—to burn or behead him, a prompter process than to refute him; besides, it is a readier way of soothing our wounded vanity or avenging an affront to our intellectual pride. Why take the trouble to gore a man with the horns of an intellectual dilemma, when you can impale his body at once on the stake? Why rack him with logical torture, when you can break him alive on the wheel? Why weary yourself with philosophies and philologies and the labor of reasoning, when the thumbscrew, the scourge, the shears, and the glowing brand, shall show the miscreant misbeliever he is in an evil case, so much the quicker?"

Nothing sooner enervates the intellect or dwarfs the erudition of the champions of the Church, than the conscious possession of arbitrary and absolute power.—"Why strengthen myself with learned authorities, when I have a hundred thousand men to back me? Why attempt to quench heresy by argument, when I may at once snuff it out in blood? Let dissent fret itself as it may, shall it trouble me in the awful sanctuary of my palace and behind my rampart of fortresses and standing armies? Shall I bother myself with their impudent 'logical points?' Why, I have half a million of steel ones, comprehensible by the most asinine obstinacy! They refuse authority?—they want light, do they? The stupid reprobates! A little earthly flame, that shall give them a foretaste of the eternal illumination, shall dispel the darkness of their minds wonderfully."—Now nothing tends so much to indolence and an enervating security as this conscious power of the summary processes of force.

Nothing again is more fatal to truly liberal learning and intellectual vigor, than the feeling that you are *subjected* to such power; the consciousness of the duty and necessity of the *implicit submission* of faith and life to the enactments of mere unreasoning authority. The conscientious or indolent disuse of your own reason from causes above enumerated, must of itself superinduce feebleness and paralysis of it, and an indisposition to its exercise. But when that exercise becomes *nugatory*, how few will resort to it! Why plague yourself, you will reason, with patient and weary study, when you know the ultimate fruit and result of all your toil—be it never so long—is *here* readily furnished, in dogmas you are determined at last to receive; yea, which you know you *must* receive *unquestioning*, or be damned for both worlds.

Why afflict myself with reasoning, when reasoning cannot at all alter my conclusions, but can only tempt me to eternal perdition? Why annoy my head with sciences when an infallible, absolute authority has already established its unalterable ordinances for all science, physical or metaphysical, mathematical or moral? What availed optics, mechanics and geometry, against cardinals and schoolmen, to the poor wretches relying on such delusions of Satan? What had they done for Galileo, but to snare him into the wrath of God and the Church? What if they did prove that the earth moved round the Sun? *Could* the earth move contrary to the decisions of the pontiff? Was not the Copernican system a heresy? Was not that enough? Why tempt the mind with scientific demonstrations, which you know beforehand are but the illusions of the Devil? And as for the power of the confutation of heretics, what need of learning or argument for that? Had not a short-hand method been taken effectually to bring Galileo to his senses, and stop his accursed tongue and the impious movement of the earth against papal ordinance, at once? Such would naturally be the reasoning of a minister and disciple of spiritual despotism.

It is obvious such despotism must have discouraged science—made logic superfluous, and taken away from the spiritual order all the common premiums of successful learning and independent thought. Could the mind gather strength or boldness of wing, while fluttering for ever in the cage of an iron, changeless, ecclesiastic system, or struggling in the meshes and convolutions of Aristotelian subtleties?—or achieve comprehensiveness of range, while working a scholastic treadmill or gyrating like a tethered beast, round the fixture of some pontific decretal?

History does not leave us to mere inferences on these points. The disastrous influence of spiritual despotism of all kinds on the intellectual power of its ministry, is abundantly attested by facts. That of Rome on the ministers of her communion, was quickly apparent in contrast with nations of the opposite party, after the Reformation, and is gloomily apparent this hour; shading with deeper coloring the countries of her dominion, on the map of the world. The history of Ecclesiastical Literature for the last three centuries, in Spain, France, Italy and Germany, is full of melancholy proofs of this comparative deterioration and imbecility. At present I refer you only to the French church, after the expulsion of the Huguenots had taken away the stimulus of rivalry, and the necessity of self defensive effort. The security, relaxation, and haughty indolence of absolute power, ensued. The consequence was, that when the awful exigency of the eighteenth century came upon her, and the wheel and stake and Bastille could no longer silence the voice of thought, nor pontifical authority nor decrees of the Sorbonne could settle all questions of science and theology, the French church seemed utterly imbecile, and almost without a struggle trodden down in the dust by the new philosophy. The French church was dumb before its foes. Religion, in its evil hour, had no defenders. Says Macaulay, "Everything gave way to the activity and zeal of the new reformers. In France every man distinguished in letters was found in their ranks. Every year gave birth to works in which the fundamental doctrines of the Church were attacked with argument, invective and ridicule. The Church made no defence, except by *acts of power*. Censures were pronounced, editions were seized, insults offered to the remains of infidel writers; but no Bossuet nor Pascal came forth to encounter Voltaire. There appeared not a single defence of the Catholic doctrine which produced any considerable effect, or which is now remembered. A bloody, unsparing persecution, like that which put down the Albigenses, might have put down the philosophers. But the time for De Montforts and Dominics had gone by. The punishments which the priests were still able to inflict, were sufficient to irritate, but not sufficient to destroy. Orthodoxy soon became the badge of ignorance and stupidity."

Can we wonder, Christianity being left exclusively with such defenders, that infidelity had its own way with everything?

Thus despotism prepares for infidelity by intellectually enfeebling and disarming the Church.

CHAPTER VI.

SPIRITUAL DESPOTISM.

Despotism Corrupts the Spiritual Power, through Hierarchy, Confessional, Celibacy, Separation of Power from the People ; Peculiar Corruptions of Politico-Ecclesiastical Despotism, especially around the Thrones of Central Europe, in the 17th and 18th centuries—Cardinal Dubois—Regent of Orleans—Louis 15th—Christianity made a Religion of Force—Terrible pressure of Spiritual Despotism the precedent ages—Reaction as the Force applied—England and in France compared—Christianity hated of the Nations as the ally of Secular Tyranny—Infidelity from Superstition—from Infallibility. Essential and immortal malignancy of Spiritual Despotism.

We have thus far seen despotism destroying faith by its war on human reason and ecclesiastic culture. A deadlier aspect of the same evil cause now engages us. Despotism again, breeds unbelief, inasmuch as it *corrupts*, while it darkens and emasculates the spiritual power. Thus, spiritual despotism in the seventeenth and eighteenth centuries, produced infidelity, not only by mental feebleness, indolence, illiterateness in the clergy (the natural defenders of Christianity), but also still more, by generating among them a *corruption of morals* tending to repel mankind from the religion they profess to represent.

Despotism ever fouls its own instruments. Spiritual despotism does this by the relations it establishes between the grades of the hierarchy, and between the hierarchy and the people. First the intercourse of the different orders of the clergy with each other and with the laity, an intercourse of absolute authority on the one hand, with implicit obedience and servility on the other, can hardly fail to be mischievous to the morals of both; producing the vices of intolerance, ambition, arrogance, in the one relation, offset against those of abject obsequiousness, lip-homage and duplicity on the other. This is the fatal vice of absolute power. It is a double-edged curse, deadly alike to its possessor and its object. Like a cancer or conflagration, it consumes both ways, above and below. Add now to the influences springing from these relations of power, *the peculiar institution for the employment of them*, found in the Romish church, that most complete instrument for spiritual subjugation, which despotism ever invented, and at the same time the most cunning device for *corrupting* Church and society ever born of infernal guile, the *confessional!*—remember, moreover, that this institute was by the same despotism conjoined with an enforced *celibacy* of *its ministers*, and we shall not wonder at the corruption of the clergy in the Romish church in the centuries we are investigating! Indeed, the confessional is another double-edge curse; worked according to prescribed rule and question, stirring up the mind of both questioner and questioned perpetually to thoughts of evil, and pouring through the clerical mind the moral filth of Christendom! I do not see how such an institution, so administered, connected with the causes above mentioned, could fail to defile the purest order of men on earth.

Again, despotism ever tends to corrupt its minisisters, inasmuch as *they hold office and power from above,* and do not feel amenable to the common conscience and reason of mankind. They hold their position of the central despotism; which may perhaps be as often propitiated by vices as by virtues; especially if connected with that merit (countervailing in despotic administration all faults), viz. subserviency and devotion to itself. Moreover, it is the law of power in this world of ours, that in order to keep it pure, it must be in constant commerce with the great heart of humanity. Its virtue, Antæus like, must often, for its reinvigoration, touch the common earth. It must feel the heart-beat of the millions below; the pulsation of the immortal instincts of the human conscience and reason, that though often smothered, blinded, dumb, still never die; but which are born fresh with fresh human souls, in each was generation. Authority needs to feel that it is amenable to the public judgment of mankind, and must plead at the bar of public opinion. Cut off the brain from the heart, and insanity and death ensue. But this was the position of the spiritual power, in those centuries, in all Catholic, and much of Protestant Europe. Its ministers and minions held of hierarchs and kings only. They were cut off from the great heart of the world.

But corrupting as are *all* despotisms, most corrupting of all forms of them is the politico-ecclesiastical type, that associates itself so extensively with the religious history of modern Europe. This type has its peculiar viciousness, first, in the fact that it usually pours the coffers of the State upon the Church, and crushes spiritual life under State endowments. It smothers ecclesiastic virtue under a cloth of gold. The revenues of the French church for instance, before the Revolution, from tithes alone, amounting to one hundred and thirty millions of francs per annum, in addition to other numerous incomes, and those from ecclesiastical domains, (amounting to about one third of the entire soil of France)—such a revenue, guaranteed and sacred to it, utterly independent of the public reason and conscience of the nation, were enough, combined with the other causes, to ensure the corruption of any Church in the world.

A second cause of the peculiar viciousness of this type of despotism is found in the fact, that all subjects of the monarchy are of course members of the Church. The distinction between the Church and the world, is thus obliterated; both practically, and in public idea; and the nation with all its crimes, ignorance, and vices, is at once imported within the pale of the spiritual communion. We need not argue such an importation must corrupt the spiritual body that incorporates it. Indeed the very idea of religion is vitiated, if not destroyed, by it. Its moral tone must be relaxed and the standard of ecclesiastic virtue and morals universally lowered.

Another cause of infidelity in politico-ecclesiastical despotism, is found in the fact that the secular as well as the spiritual tyranny, is to be propitiated by churchmen; and that too by gratifications and flatteries addressed to the crimes and vices often of kings as well as hierarchs; and that political as well as ecclesiastical gifts and honors, are the bribes offered to the clerical order, for such gratifications and flatteries. Now, in addition to all the causes enumerated above, as vitiating the Church in the seventeenth and eighteenth centuries, let all the emoluments and offices of State and the objects of courtly cabal and faction, be thrown forward as prizes of clerical ambition and intrigue;—prizes to be sought amid the scenes and circles that surrounded the thrones of Central Europe in those ages; amid the bloody debauch of the Valois, and the putrid dissoluteness of the Bourbons; the hollow and prudish corruptions of the court of Louis XIV.; the shameless and unspeakable orgies of the regency, and the foul seraglio of Louis XV. Let *Churchmen* be obliged to jostle amid the roués, debauchees, ruffians and minions of the palace! to caress the bloody fingers of a Catharine de Medici! cater to the lusts of a Philip of Orleans, or Louis XV.! flatter a Pompadour and sue for a smile of the infamous Du Barri; to plot and purchase and slime their way to greatness through scenes and means like these, and we are not astonished that there issues forth some strange, portentous product of evil. Even cardinals like Rohan and Dubois, cease to be monsters mid the creations of such a system. Such fruit grows naturally of such roots. Nor can we wonder when we see a Church in the embrace of such despotism, civil and spiritual, filling *Europe* with infidelity by the spectacle of its corruptions.

We bring the charge, then, against spiritual despotism wedded to political—of making the eighteenth century infidel by the *corruptions it had wrought in the Church.* It had corrupted it, by the relations of power and servility it established between the different ranks of the hierarchy, and between them and the laity. It had corrupted it by the double curse of the confessional, growing out of those relations conjoined with an enforced celibate of ecclesiastics and devotees. It had corrupted the Church, by smothering ecclesiastic virtue under State endowments and sinecures, by incorporating the world with the Church and thus obliterating religious distinctions, and consequently the religious sense in society; and by mingling up ecclesiastics with all the intrigues, ambitions, cabals, and dissoluteness of regal courts, especially of the seventeenth and eighteenth centuries, in Europe. I need not argue that despotism in *corrupting* the Church, of necessity *made the nation infidel.* The avenue from ecclesiastical corruption to unbelief, yawns ever open and wide as the gates of hell.

A *tyrannous church* my mind feels cannot be from a true God. A *corrupt* one, it knows cannot be. There is no surer way of producing infidelity, than by arraying a man's natural conscience against his faith. The God and Father of his conscience, must be a God of spotless purity. Such also must be the religion emanating from him. A religion that comes burdened and foul with crimes, bringing its appeal to the tribunal of the reason and conscience, is certain, unless reason and conscience are besotted and blinded by ages of abuse, to be driven away, ignominiously rejected from that tribunal. The most terrible fountain of infidelity in all times, is a godless church. A religion coming before me with hands dyed in human gore, with stains of lust and gluttony all over its garments, and claiming as God's vicegerent to master my conscience and bind my reason and muzzle my speech, I turn away from in more than incredulity, I hate—more, I loathe, I abhor it. But such was the aspect presented before the French nation by the professed representative of Christianity in the midst of the eighteenth century. The corruptions of the French church were, during this period, unspeakably hideous. Crimes beyond nature stained the robes of its prelates; and all the crimes of common nature showed themselves with unblushing effrontery within the chancel and the oratory!

All the sacred names of offices most holy in the Romish church, appear in the foulest association on the sin-bleared, blood-blotted record of those times. Abbés, curates, priests, Jesuits, bishops, archbishops and even cardinals, are presented, in the perspective of those ages, mingled up with sins and shames whose very hideousness protects them from the vengeance of history, and permits in this place only an allusion. Nor do the meshes of intrigue, simony, and sensuality that involve such personages, isolate them: they embrace the whole French church; and with it, their web implicates, also, Rome, the pontiff, and the Romish world. This corruption goes far back, mingling ecclesiastics with the perjury and lusts, assassinations and massacre of the latter Valois. It is somewhat gilded over with a hollow, hypocritical propriety, during the latter years of Louis XIV.! though even then the splendor of Bossuet, and the purity and genius of Fénélon and Pascal, could not cover it from the sneers of the court and nation. But in the unspeakable orgies of the Regent, Philip of Orleans, who succeeded him, revenge was taken for all past restraints and compulsory proprieties, and no terms were kept longer with the moral sense of mankind. In them, a cardinal—one of the highest and most sacred dignitaries of the Romish church—of rank second only to the pope—a *cardinal* appears as prime minister, buffoon and pander of the horrid debauch; its chief figure, beside the foul and blasphemous Regent himself, sits *Cardinal* Dubois, amid scenes rivalled only by those for which God blotted out ancient Sodom. "All that we read," says Alison, "in ancient historians, veiled in the decent obscurities of a learned language, of the orgies of ancient Babylon, was equalled if not exceeded, by the nocturnal revels of the Regent, the *Cardinal* Dubois, and his licentious associates." They would exceed belief, if not narrated by the testimony of concurring eye-witnesses. To such a length did the license go, that the young Duchess De Berri—the beautiful daughter of the prince of that name, one of the noblest of France—assisted at his nocturnal revels, with his mistresses and opera dancers; and even with two of the fairest of the troop occasionally personated the three goddesses who contested the prize of beauty before the son of Priam! and in the costume too of the fable.

The Duc St. Simon, an eye-witness, in his annals, gives us sketches of these scenes. But those sketches only hint at what even the French courtier of the court of the Regent and Louis XV., blushes more fully to reveal. Even those sketches I dare not translate before you, nor dare I quote from authorities everywhere accessible.

Nor are these scenes in the history of Dubois alien from the rest of his life. His vices were notorious before he became cardinal; were the scandal of the French capital when he was a simple abbé. Spite of all these, and persevering in them all, he rises to the highest honors in the French church, and next to the highest in the Romish world. He is made Archbishop of Cambray! President of the assembly of the French church! Finally, through bribery, intrigue, and corrupt influences implicating the Romish world—extending from the supreme pontiff, to our astonishment, to such pure names as that of Massillon —through means like these, finally he is *cardinal! Crowned*, *robed*, *consecrated*, with the anointing of the sacred oil, with the investiture in Heaven's pure white!—the foul wretch leprous all over with sin! *consecrated* by the laying on of holy lands! and the sign of the blessed cross! and the invocation of the Holy Spirit! and the awful names of the Father, the Son and the Holy Ghost! *consecrated*, in the presence of hierarchs and princes! amid the solemnly sworn teachers and guardians of our holy religion, and in the delegated and constructive presence of the High Priest of Catholic Christendom! *consecrated* a *Cardinal Bishop of the Romish world!!* Such a consecration! Need we ask what made France and the world infidel? Such a consecration! It were enough to send a hoot through Pandemonium. A consecration like this might smite a century with infidelity.

True, all cardinals were not like the hideous Dubois;—nor were they ostentatious libertines and voluptuaries, like Rohan; nor were all archbishops like the scandalous Archbishop of Arles, or the infamous Bishop of Sisteron, or like the intriguant and infidel Bishops Bissy, Tencin, and Tressan, or like the Bishop of Tours, of whom the witty Richelieu says, "He ought to have been bishop of but one city, which should have been resuscitated for him—and that was Sodom." Nor were all nuncios like the licentious and brutal Bentevoglio. But still, though for the honor of human nature, we cannot regard them as universally representative of the French church, is not their case fearfully significant of the character of the leaders in it?—significant of the standard of the morals of that Church in which such monsters were not even strange examples, and where their appalling vices were no impediment in the attainment of the highest ecclesiastic preferments, and offices of the most awful sanctity? And what but skepticism and irreligion could spring up in the shadow of such a Church? A glance at it might suffice to answer our whole inquiry; presenting us with the incredible scandals connected with ecclesiastic history in that capital, which was at the same time the focus of infidelity and of European civilization. Nor could the manners of the Church have been amended under the successor to the Regent—a Church dragging its lawn and purple, as the French church was compelled to do, through the filth that surrounded the throne of Louis XV. with his seraglio of Vallières, Pompadours, and Du Barrés; and the unspeakable infamies of "*Parc aux Cerfs!*"—infamies rendering credible what ancient history tells us of the manners of the courts of the Seleucidæ and the Ptolemies, and of the tyrants of the Roman world: but infamies, even foul as they were, surpassed by those of the royal cousin, the Duke De Chartres, whose unnatural crimes, infamous even in those foul ages, have come down to us rather as a hideous whisper of tradition, a rumor shuddering through the last age, than in open historic record; because letters shrank abhorringly from the task of chronicling them. You will pardon me, I am sure, for not attempting to follow out more minutely in offensive detail, the ecclesiastic corruption that mingles with the stygian flood of national immorality and irreligion, flowing under the throne of the later Bourbons.

When the historian tells us that toward the latter part of the reign of Louis XV., "no one but the *king*, and the dauphin, and dauphiness evinced any respect for religion," we are not surprised. We should suppose one such specimen of a professed believer as Louis XV. was enough; as much as one age could bear! One such as this most *Christian* Majesty! himself a hoary-sensualist, "praying," as

Alison tells us, in the intervals of debauch with the youthful victims of his harem, "that Heaven might preserve their orthodox principles," and, in consequence of the numbers of these victims, which, enticed to the recesses of his seraglio, mysteriously disappeared from society, suspected by the horror-struck multitude of attempting to reinvigorate his exhausted age with a bath of human blood! One such specimen of a believer as this sick monarch, dying in full odor of orthodoxy, and in the peace of the Church, partaking of the holy communion, with mistresses of his lusts around his dying bed hardly yielding place to the administration of the awful sacrament; then buried as his most *Christian Majesty*, and panegyrized by an Abbé St. Maury with funeral eulogy, as if a confessor and exemplar of saintly virtues! One such example were enough to make the faith of a world retch! were enough to destroy all respect for the religion represented by such a Church, and to fill a realm with infidelity. One such specimen of a respecter of Christianity, all that the kingdom presented! Very probably! A corrupt kingdom might well shrink away from beside him, and leave him alone on the platform of faith he professed to occupy; in horror at his mightier foulness, and in terror lest the bolts of outraged Heaven that should strike the monster, should smite all that stood with him.

Surely a place beside Louis XV. could hardly be one of safety, if so be there was a God, and that God could ever be angry. The faith and Christianity of Louis, XV.! It is more than ridiculous, it is horrible! The sacrilegious blending of pietism with brutal sensualism in his history, appals us more than the open, sneering, Heaven-daring atheism of the Regent. It breeds infidelity, too, more surely. The world cannot believe in a religion or a Church that fellowships such scoundrels. They will not believe in God or a divine justice if its bolts strike not such examples, nor in a Hell if it be not stirred from beneath in all its depths to meet such monsters at their coming?

Despotism, again, possessing the Church, must produce unbelief, in destroying the *intellectual* and *moral prestige* of Christianity as being a religion of superior *reason*, and *logic*, and *liberty*, and *love*. As such it came at first to humanity; a kingdom of truth, and relying on truth alone as its armor and strength. But spiritual despotism makes Christianity abandon this vantage ground, and descend to the level of falsehoods. It presents it before the world as a religion of force, tyrannic repression and cruelty. But it is suicidal for a power properly, purely ideal, to renounce its natural prerogative of reason and conscience, and assume that of brute violence. A religious faith shrinking from the ground of free inquiry and pure logic, compels men to doubt. They will resent and resist coercion attempted in its name, as an absurdity in itself as well as an outrage on the conscious rights of the human soul. A Church employing it, they regard with distrust and hate, as abdicating its legitimacy, and becoming a tyranny. A system of truth, they will reason, would have no need to resort to force, no disposition to do it. Thus truth itself will be dishonored and discredited by an enforcement requisite only for a lie. Men will reject it in scorn and hate, and indignation, as obviously not of a God of reason, liberty and love.

Such were the fatal lessons of unbelief and hate which ecclesiastic despotism had for ages been teaching the nations of Europe. The time at last came when these lessons were to bear their ruinous fruit. The ultimate reaction was, we can clearly see, obviously destined to be terrible in proportion to the pressure that had borne down the human mind. Sooner or later must come the rebound. That mind under the long consciousness of outrage, must in the fullness of time rise in indignant unbelief, on the power that oppresses it, and its revenge must be terrible. The loathed and detested Church and everything associated with it, it will cast away in the day of its fierce wrath; and alas, as that Church is all the millions know of Christianity, they will cast away that too. The day at last came, and one wild cry of derision and rage, "an absurdity, a tyranny, a sham, a lie," rang from one end of Europe to the other, as the wizzened hag, bedizened over with the purple and scarlet of its ages of harlotry, was dragged by the infuriate million to the guillotine. The consciousness of ages of wrong, of attempted murder or enslavement of the human reason, of ages of blindness, darkness, agony and chains, was burning at the heart of nations, and they rose at last on Christianity itself in blind, frantic rage, with the battle-cry of "crush the wretch."

Thus despotism begat infidelity, by destroying the moral prestige of Christianity, and producing against it a tremendous reaction of the mind of the world. The reaction, as we have stated, was not unnaturally as the force applied; the atrocities and extravagances of insurrection, in proportion to the stringency of the precedent despotism. The results, hideous as they were, do not surprise us, if we measure our anticipations by this principle. The pressure of spiritual or rather Papal despotism, from the eleventh to the fourteenth century, was unspeakable. It is thus fully but truly described by Isaac Taylor in his work on Spiritual Despotism. "The power of the Church as keeper of Truth, and guardian of morals, and disposer of souls, embraced everything, provided for everything, and applied itself to the entire surface of human nature and of the social system. This despotism was at once spiritual and political, visible and invisible. Nothing could be more refined, nothing more substantial. In the highest sense which the terms admit, the Romish tyranny was absolute and universal. Men could not think or inquire even, concerning the processes of the material world and the laws of matter and motion, without treading upon ground which the Church had preoccupied. All philosophy was either heterodox or orthodox, and a man might be burned for an opinion in mechanics as well as an opinion in theology. There could be no acquisition or enjoyment of the goods of life, no marrying or inheriting, no devising, no ruling, no judging, no speaking, no feeling, no thinking, there could be no dying without the leave of the Church, or apart from its favor." Now let such a tremendous despotism as this (the voluminous historical memorials of which are thus summed up) be applied to society for ages, as was this, though latterly somewhat broken down, to the sixteenth century, and what a terrible history is epitomized in the logic of that one fact;—what woful, wrathful, manacled ages it drags along in the chain of its dire necessity! And is it not evident one of three results will take place? Either the mind of nations will be crushed into imbecility, stupor and despair (as in the case of Spain), or resisting, it will protest against the abuses perpetrated, and will resist in the name of religious reform (as in Protestant Europe), or unable to distinguish Christianity from its abuses, it will be driven to reject religion altogether (as *e. g.* in France), and the passionateness of either the reform or rejection of Christianity, will be in the ratio of the stringency and pressure of the previous despotism. As spiritual despotism had chained all science, all society, all civilization, and all humanity, it is no wonder all science, society, humanity and civilization, became infidel. Action and reaction were equal by the law of moral dynamics. Imagine such a pressure, age after age, bearing down without remission or relief; every interest, crushed; each breathing space, closed; the clutch of tyranny ever remorselessly tightening upon its victim; the soul of the world like the terrible agent pent up in the steam-engine, prisoned under ever-narrowing compress of clamp and rivet and band;—when it bursts that compress, as burst it surely will, who shall measure the ruinous passion and power of its rebound?

You will see all these principles and the multiform evils of spiritual despotism, verified in the seventeenth and eighteenth centuries of European history.

In what countries *e. g.* in Europe was it, that the transition and revolutionary periods in religion and philosophy passed with the least injury to Faith? Was it not England? that country where imperfect as her toleration was, the right of private judgment had been most asserted and vindicated, and the power of spiritual despotism most broken. The storm of infidel philosophy and sentiment beat upon her as upon France, but she stood like her own island, steadfast, amid the floods, while her neighbor on the continent seemed utterly wrecked. Why the difference? The exercise of the right of private judgment professed by Protestantism, and to some extent accorded to the English nation, together with the open Bible, had in a measure educated the national mind. It could see a Christianity *beyond the Church*, and did not identify the religion of Jesus with the corruption and tyranny, the absurdities and falsehoods of the spiritual power. Discussion, to some extent free, had been a conductor to disarm the storm; nor had the common mind such grievous wrongs to resent as in the neighboring kingdom. No religious massacres, no edicts of the exile of millions of Huguenots, had driven from her realm the confessors and principles of Church reform and spiritual freedom; leaving her to meet the storm of infidel Revolution without intelligence or piety to withstand its violence, or ability to construct a

Christian and permanent order from the ruin. No confounding, in the popular mind, of Christianity with tyranny, had made her millions frantic with rage against religion itself, and converted her revolutions into a blasphemous insurrection against God. "When the enemy came in like a flood" on the British Isles, the Spirit of the Lord, through champions disciplined in the school of Protestantism to vigorous, manly, Christian reason, lifted up a standard against it. A Chillingworth, a Barrow, a Tillotson and Leighton, an Owen, a Clark, and Baxter, a Howe, a Wilberforce, Whitfield, Wesley, Butler, and their compeers of the seventeenth and eighteenth centuries, rallied round the ark of English Faith during this perilous era, and bore it up.

Protestant England had not been free from wrongs against the right of private judgment. We forget not the Bonners, and Lauds, and Tudors, and Stuarts, and her crimson statute book bristling with acts of uniformity, nor her dark record of religious murders, and imprisonments, and exiles. But she had offended least, certainly had been least successful amid modern nations in attempts at the suppression of the right of private judgment; and she alone stood erect in the revolutionary storm. She had had no dragoonades, no St. Bartholomews, and she had no 2d of September.

In France, contrawise, spiritual despotism had

been seemingly completely successful in crushing down or expelling the elements of religious liberty and reform; had taken away the Scripture, exiled millions of Huguenots, imprisoned and silenced the Jansenists, and enchained and blinded the popular mind; consequently, she had no champions to stand by and defend Christianity against the floods of atheistic impiety that overwhelmed her.

To the awakened national mind, to Voltaire, Rousseau and the Encyclopedists, she had nothing to present but a Church that warred on enlightenment, on science, on the instinctive sentiment of rights in the soul of man, and in whose skirts was found the righteous blood of the confessors and martyrs of ages; a Church, which, incapable of repentance, brought its puerile superstitions and its cruel intolerance down into the civilization of the close of the eighteenth century. We do not excuse, and yet we do not so much wonder at infidelity and rage towards Christianity in a people, and amid philosophers knowing of Christianity only the French church of the last century. Nature, yea, the very principles of Christianity taught them to hate that hollow sham and monstrous caricature that abused its name.

Indeed the philosophers—Voltaire and his compeers, had the secret of their strength in Christian truths mingled with their errors, and truths which were valid against that Church which they mistook for Christianity. It has been truly said of them, "They were men who with all their faults, moral and intellectual, thus made manifest war on what they considered as abuses, whose blood boiled at the sight of cruelty and injustice, and who on many occasions placed themselves between the powerful and the oppressed, and while exhibiting an irrational and disgraceful rancor towards Christianity, yet had in a far greater measure than their opponents, that charity towards all classes and races, which Christianity enjoins. Religious persecutions, judicial torture, arbitrary imprisonment, slavery and the slave-trade, were the constant subjects of their lively satire and eloquent disquisitions. When an innocent man was broken on the wheel at Toulouse—when a youth guilty only of an indiscretion, was burned at Abbeville, a voice went forth from Lake Leman which made itself heard from Moscow to Cadiz, and which sentenced the unjust judges to the contempt and detestation of Europe. The really efficient weapons with which the philosophers assailed the evangelical faith were borrowed from the evangelical morality. On the one side was a Church boasting a purity of doctrine direct from the apostles, but disgraced by the massacre of St. Bartholomew's, the murder of the best of the kings, the war of the Cevennes and the destruction of Port Royal. On the other side was a sect laughing at the Scriptures, shooting out the tongue at the Sacraments, but ready to encounter principalities and powers in the cause of justice, mercy and toleration." Such a combination and antagonism could not fail to be most disastrous both to religion and humanity, both to faith and liberty. When Christianity ceased to be the champion of justice and mercy, and to lead on reform in its attacks on the sins of the times, faith perished. But without faith, humanity could not live long, and reform became of necessity the genius of ruin.

The last that we shall notice, and one of the deadliest crimes of spiritual despotism against both God and man, was its placing Christianity in antagonism to human liberty, and presenting her to the mind of nations as their oppressor. Terrible was the wrong thus wrought by her to the religious faith and the freedom of the millions, in associating Christianity with all the crimes, outrages and shames of absolute monarchy in modern Europe. She must answer at the bar of history for the fact that unbelief is so extensively the badge of liberal and reform principles, in central and southern Europe. It is she that has abused oppressed nations with the stupendous and deadly falsehood, that in loving liberty they must hate Jesus Christ, and that insurrection against Christianity must be the first step in unchaining Europe. She must answer for the general unbelief and hate toward the Christian religion that pervades the liberal party in Catholic Christendom; which this hour render the conjunction of freedom with faith and order impossible, and make the emancipation of Europe a despair for a long era. Never was there a conjunction more baleful in the horoscope of Europe, than when the despotic Church and State appeared in portentous alliance in its house of life, brandishing their shackles and their wrath not only over this world, but over the awful realms of the everlasting, subsidizing in their war on humanity, not only the terrors and pains of earthly racks and dungeons, but the anger of God, the darkness of the eternal prison, and the flames of an infinite despair. This alliance presented religion itself as bolting the dungeon doors of the nations, placing its own fiery cherubim over the gateway to the better era, and driving them from the tree of life. It was this disastrous conjunction that exhibited Christianity before the millions as coming down from the past, laden with all the sins and shames of absolute power in Europe, for ten opprobrious centuries.

But could this be—could spiritual despotism

through this alliance thus exhibit Christianity, without drawing on her the hate and execration of nations, that went up against ages of cruel oppression? Could she exhibit the Church of Jesus, thus stained all over with the lust and bloodshed of European tyrannies, baptizing their frauds, consecrating their cruelties, defending their abuses and absurdities, fawning upon their mistresses and minions, and canonizing with funeral falsehood monsters whose names, rotting before their bodies, were already reeking in the nostrils of the whole world—could she thus exhibit Christianity, the partner, the tool, the sycophant of tyrants and banded with them in their conspiracy against the liberties of mankind, without shaking the faith of the world? Does not this false presentation of Christianity by spiritual despotism furnish ample solution of the strange feature of the skepticism of the eighteenth century—strange for a thing so cold and negative as unbelief—the *rage*, not incredulity simply, but the *rage*, with which the millions rose against Christianity in the revolutionary catastrophe of its close? Does it not also furnish an explanation of the present melancholy condition of the mind of Europe, and of that infidel and anarchical democracy which the convulsions of the old world are perpetually pouring upon our shores? This disastrous consequence of the spiritual despotism of the old world in placing Christianity in a false position before the million, is one of the gravest perils of liberty as well as of Christian faith in this age, and even in this country. It is one of the most fearful difficulties of modern history. Christianity must be recognized by the nations as a *deliverer* before they can be either permanently believing or free.

I ask, then, in the close of our survey of this topic, whether in analyzing and tracing the infidelity of the eighteenth century, we have over-estimated the evil efficacy of spiritual despotism—the usurpation of authority by man over man in religious belief and worship; the claim by one or an order, of mastery over the religious faith of the million. Does it not present itself, primarily and ultimately if not immediately, as the great cause—the cause of causes, of that portentous phenomenon we have been tracing? Was it not such of necessity through its war on the right of private judgment, and consequently, on the very power or possibility of faith? such through the intellectual imbecility, the ignorance and corruption it wrought in the Church? and such through its false presentation of Christianity as a religion of force and cruelty, the enemy of human freedom, a sanctuary of fraud and lust, and the ally, accomplice and champion, of secular tyrannies? And shall we in full view of such facts, go about this question with prudish and measured phrase, and timid and hesitant suggestion, as though it involved some most difficult mystery, requiring the most profound and delicate analysis to resolve it? Inquire after the skepticism of the eighteenth century in the face of such a history? As well ask why Hell is dark when the shadow of the Devil is on it!

Much more, shall we permit pedantry and priestcraft and the minions of a spiritual despotism, in stilted and sanctimonious cant, shaking the head in oracular horror at progress and freedom, to perplex with Jesuitical twaddle of "*Protestant license and anarchy*" a question so clear as this? a question whose answer is so intuitive, that it lies back of all argument; so instantaneous, that it outstrips all process of induction, and flashes on the soul with the quickness of instinct? a question, to decide which, calls in no more a conscious philosophy, than does touch or taste, or the eye or the ear? which can be carried into the court of Logic not at all, but lies in the realm of first principles and primary instincts, that enter vitally and immortally into the constitution of the human soul? Such enormities in the name of God and Religion, casting no moral eclipse on the world! It must be because there is no light in its universe, no God in its sky! In the presence of an ecclesiastical history like this, that throws a shadow broad and black as Tartarus, to grope with affected perplexity after the *rationale* of an age of unbelief, and especially to point, in maudlin lament, or solemn and pompous dogma, at *Protestant philosophy* and *liberty* as its guilty cause!—shall we allow spiritual despotism thus to implead her antagonist for her own crimes? Make the light then creator of darkness? Day of the night! Accuse the morning of the shadow of Mont Blanc! the sun of his own eclipse! Until the laws of the human soul and the moral world are subverted, such atrocities and opprobrium with the arrogated sanction of God, must darken the earth with infidelity. Such facts and no skepticism? That were even the most hideous portent of all! A world in which such facts should cast no shadow—that, sure, were Erebus!

We ask, then, in view of the argument and history we have pursued, are we not justified in regarding religious liberty as the safeguard rather than foe, of religious faith? yea, as being the very life of religion itself? Are we not right in contending, never so jealously, against the intrusion among us of servile and absolutistic principles in spiritual interests? and the more so, the more insidious are their approaches?

We know that wearied, disgusted and affrighted

by the confusion, anarchy and revolution, that manifest themselves in the religious world, there are some among us who sigh for tranquillity as a supreme good; and almost look around for refuge, order and repose, even in the bosom of despotic authority. But we cannot, if we would, find them there! We cannot if we would, thus lay aside the responsibility of private judgment. Heaven has appointed no man, nor office, nor order, as infallible dispenser of its truth; nor has it placed any marks on minds to tell us who have the truth. Heaven gives us no guarantees against shams. Yea, it tells us the *truth* shall make us free. He that will serve, let him know, he *will serve the Devil.* No power, not of the kingdom of darkness, will accept at his hands the impious surrender of his spiritual manhood. History, moreover, arises with philosophy to warn us, it is vain to seek permanent *order* even, under the shadow of despotism. We have already seen from that shadow, chaos and ruin rushing forth over a cycle of European history. The impious children of old night are there, the anarch brood of darkness and wrath. No! Not that way at all! Not that way, but in the clear, full, and fearless assertion of Protestant freedom, in full Protestant light and liberty, lies the only way of safety for Church and society. Nor could we carry the world that other way of despotism, again, if we would; any more than we can carry back the earth in its orbit. That way is, thank God, closed up, we believe, for ever. The perils and hopes of *freedom* are before us. Through freedom we are to be saved, or through freedom to be lost, for both worlds. Nor will we shrink back from the responsibility, vast and solemn though it be: from the perils inseparable from the hopes of liberty. These perils—the perils of movement and change—are in the great necessities of progress. They are in God's great order of life. We accept them thankfully, and on the whole, fearlessly. To us, life (the life of liberty) is the most beautiful and beneficent of things, or at least, nothing seems beautiful without it. From a world without it, we flee; our pulse beats low and our breath grows difficult in its presence. Its uniformity oppresses, its very order is a torture. We pray not, then, that the air be prisoned, though of its freedom be born the tempest! We would not bar up the river, though its free stream inundates the harvest, or bears the unwary to the cataract! We would not chain up the ocean, though I know ruin oft rides on its free and stormy wave! I would not the wheel of the great globe were stopped, though I know its free orbit bears through frost and fire. No! free flow the river! free walk ye winds the boundless air! roll on in thy glorious freedom, O sea! free be thy wheel, O earth, through thy starry zone! for in your freedom, there is life and beauty, music and joy! Take away free movement and all things sicken, grow feeble, sad and foul. The skies afflict us with their eternal changelessness. The stars glare out from the stagnant infinite, like the staring eyes of the dead. An agony of suffocation is on the air. Nature's great heart-beat is stifled, and her vital currents curdle; universal life gasps and faints under the vast asphyxia. Yea, take away its free motion, and the eternal vault collapses! this universal organism goes into dissolution. So with regard to the world of religious faith and order; chain up its movements and you slay them. Repress the changes of life, and those of death will enter. The attempt to conserve them by the stereotype of despotism, is like attempting to keep the beauty of the body immortal by sealing it with the fixedness of death. Under that marbleized beauty, invades the worm. Decay, corruption, dissolution—these are the sure foredoomed changes of that which under these heavens assumes to be the changeless. Order in the social and religious world is a thing not of mechanism, but of life. It endures, not by stereotype, but by growth and progress. The march of Humanity and Christianity henceforth, is not to be taken between the alternatives of *despotism with order* on the one hand, and *liberty with danger* of *anarchy* on the other; but between two banners, the one unfolding to the free winds its motto, "*Liberty with Hope, Life with Change, Progress with Peril;*" while in letters of night, stretches across that other way of humanity the blazon, "*Absolutism with Anarchy, Tyranny with Torpor, Despotism with sure Decay, Despair, Death.*"

CHAPTER VII.

FRANCE.

France the most Powerful Generator and Diffuser of Infidelity—Her Position in Modern History—The Model Kingdom of Europe—Oracle of Civilization—Her Early Culture—Genius—Language—Court Literature—Political Ascendency—Self-diffusiveness—Causes of Infidelity in her Civil and Ecclesiastic Constitution and History—Religious Wars—Albigenses—Huguenots—Separation of the Actual from the Ideal the widest—Reaction of Repressed Mind most Passionate—Daring and Revolutionary Despotism in France in the 17th and 18th Centuries—Absolutism of Louis XIV.—Its Mischief—Two Great Crimes of the French Church and Monarchy Generative of Infidelity—Ecclesiastic Barbarism extending down toward the close of the 18th Century—Torture and Execution at Abbeville 1776—Despotism in France applied to a Mind the most Active, Daring, Witty and Philosophic in Europe.

In our view of the great defection of the human mind from Christianity in the seventeenth and eighteenth centuries, we have thus far been engaged for the most part, with causes and principles of general and well-nigh of universal scope, throughout Christendom during this era. We now propose, in further illustration and analysis of our theme, to look more narrowly at the *geographic centre and focus of the plague.* That view will develop important principles in relation to the laws of its origin and propagation.

In illustration and enforcement of general principles thus far considered, it has been seen that our constant fountain of instances is French history and society. We now propose to direct attention especially to that fountain, France itself; and consider her especial efficiency in producing the sad phenomenon we are investigating.

Eminent amid the causes of the spread of skepticism over Europe in the seventeenth and eighteenth centuries, stands forth the prominent and commanding position of France in European civilization during that period.

France was in those ages the most powerful elaborator and diffuser of infidelity, as she was the most powerful elaborator and diffuser of all elements of civilization. The French mind was the most active in Europe—the most generative, the most diffusive. Thoughts, feelings, ideas, sentiments, manners went forth from Paris to the possession of Europe.

The causes of this position of France in modern civilization radicate back to the birth of modern Europe. The municipal remains of ancient civilization, proximity to the scenes where ancient literature and art lingered longest and were earliest revived, the rise of the Frank Empire earliest amid political or at least national and imperial forms after the fall of the Roman Empire, were among the originating influences. Subsequently, Provençal culture, the earlier consolidation of the French Monarchy and formation of the French Court, with the most brilliant and perfect development of chivalry and feudalism, the magnificence of baronies and baronial courts and their subsequent focalization in that of royalty, the agitation and collision of the parties in the era of the Reformation and their final equipoise in the pacification of Nantes—these causes conspiring perhaps with the livelier genius of the French mind, had contributed to give to that mind a culture more mature, refined, productive and energetic than any other in Western or Central Europe. And not only was the French mind the most prolific of ideas, but from influences hereafter to be specified, it was the most likely of all to reflect the skeptical genius of the age.

The above causes of earlier culture and of finer and livelier energy in the French mind, tended with other influences to make France also *the most powerful diffuser* of her civilization, whatever it might be. To this result conspired moreover the distinctive personal genius of brilliant and powerful monarchs.

Thus, in consequence of all these causes, in France earliest amid the nations of modern Europe, the regal court having absorbed the baronial, coercing or alluring the noblesse from their fastnesses to the Capital, Paris had become France, and France under the Valois and Bourbons, had become the metropolis of civilization itself; the model kingdom of Europe; the most consolidated, powerful, brilliant and courtly amid its monarchies, and with a type of culture the most polished and cosmopolite. She was leader in the literary, social and political realm; the standard of taste, manners, literature and philosophy as well as of civil and military administration and of diplomacy. Her genius was mistress in saloons and academies, in the cabinet and on the field of battle. What was French was sure to become European. A peculiar vivacity and polish had given a peculiar diffusiveness to her intellectual and social culture. Her Court became the mirror of gallantry and gaiety, of wit and grace, and of brilliant and elegant dissoluteness. Under the corrupting though splendid rule of Francis I. and Henry IV. the vigorous and sagacious administration of Richelieu, and especially by the magnificence of arts and arms under the ambitious Louis XIV., she had been conducted forward almost to the attainment of universal empire, not only in politics but in civilization.

A galaxy of great men, brilliant generals, statesmen, courtiers and ecclesiastics, of poets, orators and philosophers, illustrates the seventeenth and eighteenth centuries in France; but they gather especially in a sidereal coronal around the throne of the grand Monarque. It will suffice to name a Condé, Turenne, Colbert, Louvois, Villars, Luxembourg, among statesmen and generals the first of the age; and allude to the genius of a Corneille, Molière and Racine, in the drama; a La Fontaine, Des Cartes, Boileau, Malebranche and Boyle in philosophy; or a Bourdaloue, Fénélon, Bossuet and Massillon, in sacred eloquence; all of these, and hosts of others of world-wide fame, constellating round the reign of Louis XIV. During the eighteenth century, Paris became the intellectual, social and political captial of Christendom; Versailles, the supreme court of European culture. The French language, with its facile, insinuating, conversable genius became every where the common medium of intercourse for the courtly and the learned; the French monarch, the most perfect and brilliant example of absolute power, the study and model of all despots. In short to an extent never equalled by any other nation in modern times, France became the oracle of civilization.

We have to add also to the above causes of the

peculiar diffusiveness of French civilization in the eighteenth century, the centrality of her geographic position, placing her among and between the most powerful European States; and also the peculiar complaisance and sympathy, the versatility, sociability and geniality, of the French mind; which seem to have distinctively marked it all through modern history, and have made it the most self diffusing in Europe; insomuch that Guizot states truly "It is necessary wherever an idea is born, it should pass through the medium of the French mind in order to take possession of Europe."

All the above causes combined to make France in the eighteenth century—what Guizot terms her, "the centre and focus of modern civilization;" and predetermined the universal spread of any social distemperature arising within her; evidently, taking possession of the French mind, it must make the tour of the continent.

But while France thus was a most effective self-diffuser, it was the calamity of modern history, that she was, at the same time, of all the nations of Europe, the most powerful elaborator and generator of religious skepticism. She was so through her history and society; through her Church, her court, and her literature.

Let us look at the relations of some of these elements of her civilization to the unbelief of the age. We shall find, that while she is the model and oracle of European civilization, she at the same time *exhibits in herself most of the various causes we have already discussed, of the infidelity of the eighteenth century, existing in their most effective and virulent type.*

Her history must have been a prolific fountain of infidelity. Her page of religious wars and persecutions, from the crusade against the Albigenses to the expulsion of the Huguenots, was amid the foulest and bloodiest in Europe; bleared over with perjury and cruelty, assassination and massacre. She had during the period of the Reformation been convulsed and torn for generations by religious wars. From the sins, shames and treacheries, the hypocrisies, fanaticisms and atrocities, of those wars, abusing the name of God and Christianity, and breeding a disgust and horror at religion from the frightful dissoluteness of manners springing from them and from the moral collapse or relaxation following them—from all these causes sown in her history, must have sprung a woeful harvest of incredulity and hate toward religion.

Two great specific crimes in her history, most ruinous to French faith, we shall have occasion to notice presently. We now refer, in general, to her religious history, as peculiarly productive of infidelity.

In France, again, the reaction of the human mind against the ages of intellectual enslavement which Europe had suffered, had been most passionate, excessive and anarchical, in her the revolution in philosophy had wrought most mightily and successfully in science; but in the realm of religion, had run a course most wild, daring, impious and ruinous. Here under the pressure of a triple despotism over politics, religion and science, the severance of speculation from affairs had been widest; the ideal and the actual most violently forced asunder; and here in consequence the shock of their rebound and collision was destined to be the most terrible to the order and faith of society.

In France, moreover, Mammonism had exhibited its climacteric of fever and delirium. In her was the most complete dethronement of the religious idea and most absolute supremacy of that of wealth. In her the money mania had wrought its wildest and maddest excesses; had most demoralized society, and brought it nearest to dissolution.

These effects manifested themselves—not because France was worst or lowest in the scale of European nations; certainly, not because of intellectual and moral imbecility. In these respects other states fell far below her. The above causes of irreligion operated in France with peculiar malignancy, because in her case there was a peculiar intellectual and moral activity of the nation, combined with inertness, corruption and imbecility of the religious power. There was life the most intense, passionate and energetic, beating in the heart of France; but life without religious illumination or control; a life on which pressed a tremendous despotism of force, and toward which the Church exhibited simply repressive acts of power, not the influences of principle, reason and truth. When those acts of power became impotent to enforce submission, as they ultimately did, the very impotency of their attempted tyranny irritated and provoked the excesses they could not restrain. With some other Catholic States there was no abnormal action, because there was not action at all; there was no fever, no spasm, no delirium, because the national mind had been stifled to long syncope, if not to death. The same blow of power which had stunned them, had however only made France blind and frantic. Tyranny which does not kill, maddens. The more crushing it be this side death, the more it maddens. In France it had reached that limit and only that. In Spain it seems to have passed it. By all these facts, France was a prolific generator of infidelity. Amid them all, the great cause of causes, the one back of all, as previously shown, was DESPOTISM—the joint tyranny of Church and monarchy, extending over almost all life and every interest.

Let us now look at the position of that cause in France, at the close of the seventeenth century. We shall see if our former reasonings were correct, France must have been a fearful elaborator of unbelief, through her *politico-ecclesiastical despotism.*

Her absolutism was the most absolute in Europe—most absolute in Church and State. Her imperious Louis XIV. had become, to use his own language, "the State," and he might have added, the Church, too. For between him and his will, he brooked not baron, or prelate, or pope. In this arbitrariness of will, he was the Henry VIII. of French History. At least, if not ordaining himself expressly, as the supreme oracle of religious faith, to his subjects, he showed himself the most absolute enforcer of the spiritual despotism, which he chose to constitute or admit; whether of the pope or of the Gallic church. Church and State were bound in adamant to his throne; though it was adamant draped and lacquered over with purple and gold. The most iron absolutism was maintained, over the realm of politics and religion. In these realms an omnipresent censorship, and espionage, watched and punished all free thought; at least, all that seemed to have any practical bearings on the outward form of Church and State. Parliament and estates, baronial prerogatives and provincial, and municipal privileges, all breakwaters of despotism, were broken down before the march of absolute power. The Huguenots that had withstood it, had been ruthlessly driven out, bearing to other lands their resentment and despair, and their millions of men and money. The Jansenist, seemingly worn out with persecutions, had been smothered in prisons, or were repenting in exile. The blood of Saint Bartholomew, if it was the seed of the Church of its martyrs, was a slow seed. For a long time that bloody stroke of despotism seemed to have accomplished its cruel end; to have slain, well-nigh, whatever elements there were of civil and religious liberty and reform, in the French nation. Seen as we now see it, it was a murderous stroke at the very life of France, that was to be awfully avenged. Protestantism was in time to come forth from its bloody grave, the Nemesis of Revolution. Smothered Jansenism was to break out anew in the plagues of skepticism and irreligion; and from Saint Bartholomew's fatal day, were to go forth the avenging furies, that should at last drag Church and monarchy, and the nation itself, under the guillotine.

But for the time, it seemed as if these stupendous

crimes had been successful, and the triumph of despotism, spiritual and political, seemed hideously complete. Not a tongue dared wag against it, in all the realms of France. There it stood, spiritual despotism wedded to political, armed with the strength and genius, the vast military force, and the iron absolutism of the mightiest, most brilliant, most imperial monarchy in Europe; the banners of olden glories floating over its battlements; the muses of grace, beauty, and pleasure, waiting in its palaces; genii of wit and song, and eloquence and victory, chained to its throne; and the swords of the heroic and the mighty, keeping watch and ward around it. The cry and the curse of the millions far below, could not rise to its heaving. The voice of the confessors of spiritual and political liberty, had sunk with their blood down to the silent depths of the earth, no more to rise. It seemed the absolute triumph of absolute despotism; despotism over State and Church; over all acting, all speaking, all thinking; political, ecclesiastical or theological. And what provinces did not these terms then embrace?

But was it absolute, was it final? Nay. Its very brilliancy was its hectic of decay. So much genius could not live with so much despotism. Its very completeness was a sure sign of its fall; unless indeed, humanity was utterly stifled below it. For down in the dark and foul depths below that splendor, the million crushed, scourged, gagged, blinded, still breathed. The fever of life and all life's fiercest lusts, still rioted in its veins; nor had its mangled eyes altogether forgotten the light they had once beheld.

Now need we repeat our argument of a former chapter, to prove that France with such a political and ecclesiastical absolutism, must have been a prolific generator of infidelity? A despotism, that by its repression of mind in the paths of the practical, drove it into wild, unrestrained, licentious speculation in the realms of the ideal; that by its war on private judgment struck at reason itself, and all power of belief; made timid and feeble, when it could not destroy the faith of nations; and rendered the Church intellectually imbecile, by forbidding the exercise of the free intellect, by taking away the necessity of argumentative conflict or defence, by bestowment of the power of force, and by removing the premiums on erudition, discovery or scientific and logical culture; a despotism that corrupted the church with gold and security, with indolence, ambition, servility and arrogance, by placing authority in connexion with tyrannic power, and cutting it off from the moral sense of mankind; corrupted it, by incorporating the world with the Church; thus confounding religious ideas, and obliterating religious distinctions among mankind; that corrupted it by applying to it the pestilent curse of celibate and confessional, and by draggling its robes through the cabal and conspiracy, the intrigue, sycophancy and debauch, of dissolute courts, and jostling it with their parasites, placemen, ruffians, mistresses, and minions! a despotism, that stripped Christianity of its moral prestige as a religion of superior truth, reason and love; changed it to one of force, malignancy, and tyranny; and made it the enemy of human liberty, and the accomplice and champion of all the crimes and scandal, cruelties and oppressions of the civil tyrannies of modern Europe; and finally a despotism that invested the Church with the armor of infallibility, as a mail of burning steel, sheathing up all its future with the lies and crimes of all its past, stereotyping each error, each folly, each sin, each shame, of its history, however dim, distant, guilty or gloomy, for ever past all repentance or amendment, to the astonishment, abhorrence and execration of all time! Could a despotism, working all this in France for ages, fail of darkening, if not utterly destroying the faith of the nation? Was not France, therefore, by the necessity of its political and ecclesiastical despotism, developed in our previous argument, sure to become a fearful laboratory of infidelity? Having traversed the ground both in fact and logic, in a previous chapter, we need not stop here to go over it again.

But the curses of her despotism did not stop here. It led her into acts and measures for the repression or extinction of dissent, which made her Church a hissing and abhorrence for a century, to all the enlightened and thinking of Europe. Especially two stupendous crimes it led her to perpetrate, that proved two deadly wounds in her own bosom, gushing with gore and the poison of unbelief, over centuries and kingdoms. Those two great crimes by which she thought to purchase security and immobility, are now clearly seen to have embarked her on a wild, dark, and bloody sea, over which she was to drift for ages with no God in her sky.

The two great crimes of the French church and monarchy in enforcement of spiritual despotism, the massacre of St. Bartholomew, and the exile of the Huguenots, it is now clearly seen, avenged themselves in the destruction of both. They were suicidal to French faith, French royalty, and French liberty, at the same time; blood-blotches on her history, destined, as we now see, to spread over the pages of at least two centuries. Terrible mistakes were they, as well as crimes. They exterminated from the realm of France, those who alone might have reformed both Church and State, before the irrepressible wrath of the nation broke forth in the fire blast of the revolution.

In one of these acts, from forty thousand to fifty thousand, according to the most reliable historians, of the noblest and most enlightened of the nation, were butchered in France and the provinces in one day, in the midst of profound security, through the diabolic treachery of the court, instigated beforehand by Jesuit and priest, and congratulated and celebrated afterwards by the pope ordering Te Deums to be sung for it, in the churches in the capital of Catholic Christendom.

By the other, the revocation of the edict of Nantz in the single province of Languedoc, one hundred thousand were put to death under military execution; of whom a tenth part, at least, suffered from the frightful torments of the stake and wheel. Four hundred thousand at least fled the kingdom, and an equal number perished of famine, plague, imprisonment, the galleys and the scaffold. The faith of one hundred thousand more at least, was crushed down in tears and agony and blood, into recantation, and the silent smouldering hate of ages.

The Duc St. Simon, a Catholic, and one of the courtiers of Louis XIV. and an eye-witness of the atrocious execution of the royal edict, thus narrates; "by this edict," says he, "without the slightest pretext, without the slightest necessity, was one fourth of the kingdom depopulated, its trade ruined, the whole country abandoned to the avowed public pillage of dragoons; the innocent of both sexes were devoted to punishment and torture, and that by thousands. * * * * The world saw crowds of their fellow creatures proscribed, naked, fugitive, guilty of no crime, yet seeking in foreign lands an asylum from the cruelty of their own; which meantime was subjecting to the lash and the galleys the noble, the opulent, the aged, the weak, the delicate and those not less distinguished by their rank than their piety and virtue; and this for no reason but their religion. Still further to increase the horror of these proceedings, every province was filled with perjured and sacrilegious men; who were forced to recant. In truth such were the horrors produced by the combined operation of cruelty and obsequiousness, that within twenty-four hours, men were frequently conducted from the torture to abjuration, and from abjuration to the communion table; attended in both generally by the common executioner." Thus far St. Simon.

Now we ask does not this record point to one fearful fountain at least of the evil we are tracing? Do not the infidelity and revolution of the eighteenth century gush out of these two great repressive measures of the French church and monarchy? In the first place, could any nation in Europe have borne at that day such a bleeding of its purest, noblest, most gifted blood, its martyr, heroic, sainted blood, without moral exhaustion and paralysis, and without dooming its future to a reactive paroxysm of fever and delirium? Could the provinces, as St. Simon describes, "be filled with perjured men, one hundred thousand or more, that had passed from the gibbet and wheel to the communion attended by the public executioner," without the spreading as Alison asserts, of "the poison of infidelity and irreligion throughout the realm of France?"

Again, could the unspeakable atrocities of the dragonnades of Louis XIV., according to the statement of a Catholic courtier of that monarch, depopulating one fourth of France, pillaging provinces, devoting the innocent of both sexes—the aged, the delicate and the noble—to the scourge and the torture by thousands, driving into exile or crushing into recantation fifteen hundred thousand persons—could this take place in the light of the close of the seventeenth century, without drawing down upon the Church, in whose name they were perpetrated, and on religion itself, as far as the Church was regarded as its representative, the indignant and scornful incredulity of mankind? Could history remember the noble Coligni, his white hair dragged in blood, his heroic form mangled with murder, and trodden the livelong day of ruffian feet in the streets of Paris —or the infuriate Charles of Valois screaming through the awful tumult of the carnage from the windows of the Louvre, "Kill, kill!"—or the complot of the Tiger-Cat of Florence with Jesuit fraud weaving meshes for the trusting victims;—could history remember all these—much more the Te Deums from the religious capital of the Catholic world! and by order of its supreme pontiff! that went up as thanksgiving to Jehovah at the tidings, as if an orison of murder to the Aztec war-god! could history ever remember these without something of that shudder of horror that thrilled through nations at the time, at the dreadful rumor of those atrocities, and without breathing a chill of skepticism over all the realms of Catholic faith where Romanism was synonomous with Christianity?

We direct attention to this record in French history with no pleasure, nor with a wish to bring odium on any communion repenting of its past sins; but truth to our theme points to these as part of the terrible causes of the terrible phenomenon we are analyzing. "Hence was it," says Alison, "that philosophy confounding religion with atrocities perpetrated in its name, became imbued with skepticism, and the cause of human emancipation became synonymous in general opinion with the overthrow of Christianity."

But indeed the French church would not let history forget if she would, her complicity in the atrocities of the past. That Church brought down into the light of the latter half of the eighteenth century the torture and cruel punishments of barbarous ages, and that for the merest indiscretions. For an insult offered in a drunken frolic to a wooden crucifix, on a bridge in Abbeville, in 1776, a youth of sixteen or seventeen years of age, son of an ancient family in the magistracy, was first put to the torture, then had his tongue cut out, and was finally beheaded. And this scene in the age of Chatham and Burke—under the same sun that looked down on a Pitt, Franklin and Washington, in open sight before the wits and theophilanthropists of the Encyclopedia! Can we wonder or regret that the indignant sarcasm of Voltaire transfixed the Church guilty of such abominable cruelty and impaled it for the derision and hate of all Europe? or that the million with its great human heart felt there was quite as much religion in the humanity of the skeptic as in the pitiless fanaticism of the ecclesiastic?

For French irreligion then—the fountain of unbelief to Europe—we must arraign the French church in both its theory and practice. But that disastrous theory and practice flow directly from the spiritual despotism incorporated in it. Its tyrannous principles and its revolting history emanate directly from that dark fountain. Spiritual despotism, through the French church, must be arraigned then at the bar of history for the great apostasy of the seventeenth and eighteenth centuries.

Thus we shall find the double despotism of France in the seventeenth and eighteenth centuries preparing an era of unbelief in that kingdom. Especially by the *repressive measures* to which the alliance of spiritual and political absolutism tempted the Church, we have found unbelief and hatred of the Church, and of Christianity, which it represented, of necessity generated in the French nation.

Thus was France a terrible elaborator and evangelist of infidelity; not only by the essential genius of all despotism over faith, and especially of a despotism like hers; but she was especially so, by the peculiar measures she took to enforce that despotism; measures which the human mind in its native inextinguishable moral sense, could not but feel were as alien from a God of truth and mercy, and purity, as Hell from Heaven. The eternal instincts of the human soul must be extinguished before a religion consecrating such horrors could be forced down the throat of humanity, even though throttled and well-nigh stifled in its own gore! Voltaire's Dictionary of Philosophy, Helvetius's System of Nature, Paine's Age of Reason, the Encyclopedia—they were terrible Gospels of unbelief, but what were they all to the history of France herself! It was in itself an encyclopedia of irreligion and infidelity. More fatal to faith than the sneers and sophisms that hissed and glittered over Europe from Lake Leman, more terrible than the eloquence of the Gironde or the rage of the Mountain, was that volume written, like the scroll seen of Ezekiel, "all over within and without with mourning, lamentation and woe."

But in order to estimate the power of France as a generator of unbelief, we have to add to the above necessary tendencies of despotism, the condition of the French mind at this time, to which this despotism was applied. It was arresting a Niagara in its rapids. We have said above, the triumph of despotism seemed to be complete. It was far from being so It could not become so without, we will not say slaying the mind of France, but without a massacre of half of its population. It had not begun its work soon enough, or prosecuted it ruthlessly enough, bloody as it had been. It required the Inquisition and Philip II. and Spanish fanaticism to accomplish the work. Nor could these even have effected it for perpetuity. Now we are to bear in mind, this absolute repression of French thought and speech in the direction of State and Church, *i. e.* in the direction of the great practical and visible interests of society, was attempted on a mass of mind, if not the freest, the most licentious and volatile and vivacious, the most active, daring and irrepressible, in Europe—mind, which had felt most profoundly the stroke of the Reformation, and had sympathized deeply with that insurrection against the despotism of the spiritual power; which in art, science, brilliant culture and general literature, stood foremost amid western nations; and which had entered with peculiar enthusiasm and success on the paths of free speculation and discovery, opened by the emancipation of the European intellect from the Aristotelian and Scholastic system, and by the application of the Baconian and Cartesian methods to science. No nation had felt the impulse, religious and philosophic, of the age, more profoundly. Massacre and exile had not quenched that impulse, but only removed those who would have enlightened, tempered and guided it. It left it wild, blind, guideless, and faithless. Despotism could not annihilate the force that had been generated. Its suppression could only stop the relief movement of progress, shut down the safety-valve and bind the terrible power within, with rivet and clamp and bar! could it fail to make explosion in time, inevitable and terrible? Despotism over such a mass of mind it is evident could hardly be permanently successful, short of absolute extermination. Short of that, it would certainly madden it. You could not stop the mind's thinking, you might make thought perverse; if you put out its true lights, it would be certain to chase false ones. Arrest the natural outblow salutary to life, it will be sure to break out in ulcers or rush back in fever on the heart or in delirium on the brain. Such was the achievement of spiritual despotism in France; she struck at Heresy; she slew Faith! She shut against the nations the temples of Truth. They prostrated themselves in delirium before lies! She covered from them the face of Jehovah. They rushed to the shrines of Moloch and Mammon and of No-God! She plunged the nation into the skepticism of ignorance—or of denying Christianity from not knowing what it is. They rushed in frantic rage against that Church that abused the name of Christ and Christianity from knowing too well what *it* was. The sad truth is, France was without a knowledge of true Christianity. A despotic, cruel, superstitious Church had barred out spiritual illumination, had wrested from the millions the Bible, forbidden the free exercise of reason on matters of faith, bloodily repressed all questioning of its own authority, legislation, or institutes, and forced itself on the formal acceptance of mankind as being truly representative of Christ and His Gospel. Itself, with all its hollow pretence and hypocrisy, its corruptions and debauchery, its frauds and puerilities, stood before the philosophic, scientific and witty mind of France as the embodiment of the Christian religion. The Church standing thus—a defeature on the age, an offence to its intelligence and conscience, a foe to liberty and progress, was of course abandoned of the French mind. It turned from it in loathing and contempt. Alas it derided and cursed Christianity itself. And we can hardly wonder, if this was all the Christianity it knew. And such it was to the millions of France. Indeed even Voltaire was profoundly ignorant of the Scriptures and the Faith against which he directed the sneer of all Europe. So were many of his followers.

Morell gives very truly the process of French infidelity, and fitly defines it when he calls it the "Infidelity of ignorance."

But though ignorant of Christianity and the Bible, the French literati were learned in science, and acute and comprehensive in philosophic analysis; and they could feel and show the discrepancies of science with the teachings of the Church. So here again spiritual despotism begat unbelief; not only by errors and falsities into which all may fall, but by the fact that she could never retract or repent. Every absurdity was eternized by her infallibility. Thus she was compelled to array science against Christianity. In Protestant countries spiritual despotism escaped this consequence, because of its logical inconsistency. It abjured all claim to the infallibility that should accompany a vicegerency of Heaven; while at the same time, it arrogated the power and authority attaching only to such infallibility. Strictly speaking, it was more tyrannous, but at the same time less mischievous, in the Protestant than the Romish communion, because of its illogicalness. The former may repent—the latter, a terrible consistency petrifies to the derision and execration of all the future. This her impeccableness, binding her to not only the defence of, but to persistency in all the past, in the presence of the French mind of the eighteenth century, must have been a fearful generator of unbelief and irreligion.

CHAPTER VIII.

FRANCE.

French Literature of the 18th century—Infidel Writers and Savans—Mission of Infidelity organized—Its Apostles and Evangelists, Voltaire, Rousseau, and the Encyclopedists—Their Quarry, the French church—Its Corruption, Ignorance, Superstitions and Cruelties—Jesuitism—Its Exposé and Fall—Money-madness in France—The Primal Fountain of her Infidelity—Politico-Ecclesiastical Despotism.

IT was again the application of spiritual despotism to the French mind, such as we have above described that produced the portentous birth of the FRENCH LITERATURE of the eighteenth century; a birth as strangely mighty and wicked as those from the misalliance of the sons of God with the daughters of men, in the early world; giants in power and in impiety.

We note then France as especially an elaborator of infidelity through her literature, which literature was her protest against spiritual despotism.

Most terrible amid its legion of mischief, was that infernal birth which despotism had begotten on the French mind; at first, in driving that mind, as we have before noticed, from all qnestions of Church or State, and existing institutions, under the wand of this despotism. The policy of iron absolute repression in these directions, was attempted on a national mind the most stimulated, active, and in many walks, the furthest advanced in Europe. It could not fail to produce strange and portentous results. Obstructed in its old paths, it was impelled the more fiercely into tortuous and erratic ones. Divorced from the healthful restraints of the present and the actual, it plunged with boundless extravagance into the realms of the speculative and ideal. It avenged its tyrannous exclusion from certain fields, by frantic license in those left open. It might not touch directly faiths and institutions. It mined under all. Priest and king were prescribed to it. It rushed the more madly on the primal truths of philosophy, morality, religion and government; and wreaked its resentment for the cruelties, absurdities, the bloody and drivelling superstitions, enforced by the double tyranny above, by, first a covert doubt, and, finally, a frantic rage against Christianity and God himself. The Church had sown the wind, and she was to reap the whirlwind. The wrongs of ecclesiastic power arrogating to be Christianity in the previous centuries, its puerilities and mummeries, its outrages on common reason and conscience, were to bear their bitterest fruit in the eighteenth century; first in the literature of France, then the commanding one of the world; at last, the sown dragon's teeth were to spring up as armed men. The mind of France mistaking Romanism for Christianity, rose against religion in strange ferocity. The most brilliant genius of France was combined and organized in this dreadful warfare. The Abbé Raynal contributed the charms of historic eloquence and painting, caricaturing priests and Christianity, and embellishing a seductive naturalism; D'Alembert threw into the cause the genius whose wondrous, clear-eyed, comprehensive vision, had traced the mysteries of the modern analysis; the prodigious and varied erudition, and graceful taste of Helvetius, Diderot, and their compeers, argued, embellished and insinuated the most frightful irreligion, and most revolting sensualism. The novels of Crebillon, and Le Clos, Louvet's memoirs and innumerable madrigals, with appliances, to the public mind, of licentious adventures, voluptuous paintings, erotic sonnets, and undisguised obscenities, labored in the same evil gospel of materialism. "Such was the influence of writers of this school," says Alison, "that almost the whole philosophical and literary writings of France for a quarter of a century before the Revolution, were infidel. When David Hume was invited to meet a party of eighteen of the most literary men in the French capital, he found to his astonishment that he was the least skeptical of the party. He was the only one present who admitted even the probable evidence of the Supreme Being." If such was the religious eclipse in the realm of literature, we shall hardly wonder that the darkness spread over all the land.

Thus the curse of despotism, combining such terrible repression with so much life, necessitated this erratic, infidel, and finally anarchical career of mind. That literature that, amid the peacock pageant and hollow prudery of the model despotism of Europe—that of Louis XIV.—displays itself on that "extraordinary Parnassus where," according to Menzel, "Apollo in the pedantic bagwig, led with his fiddle the concert of frizzed and powdered muses, disguised in bodices with hoop-petticoats," and where "of the ancient motto of French chivalry—God, the king, honor and the ladies—only God and honor were left out"—that literature we do not wonder at seeing throw off those hollow proprieties and hypocritic pruderies as soon as the model despot was cold in his grave, and ministering in utter shamelessness in the Circean revel of the Regent. Nor are we surprised at finding that having passed from prudery to revel, it now passed from revel to rage; and in the

Moloch orgies of revolution, appeared a genius of ruin; scattering phrenzy and flame through cathedral and palace, where ages before it exhibited its servile and hollow mummeries. The change from the prude and hypocrite to the wanton and blasphemer, was a necessity of literature under such a despotism applied to such a national mind.

Nor can we wonder that infidelity *breaking forth as a pestilence from France as its central focus overspread Europe;* especially, when we remember how in her, infidelity became organized as a *mission*, and who were the great apostles, and who the evangelists of that mission!

Probably the earth never saw a more powerful or brilliant combination of intellects, nor one united in a more portentous project, than those who in the eighteenth century conspired for the overthrow of Christianity. They labored in their terrible work with the splendor and passion, the genius and hate of a cohort of fallen angels. Paris was the origin and centre of this conspiracy; France its first theatre. But from Paris its meshes spread through Europe.

The chief of this conspiracy, Voltaire, was one of those wondrously gifted men that seem sent of Heaven, now in mercy, and now for punishment, among mankind. His genius quick, acute, vigorous, subtle and infinitely versatile, was armed with a sense of the ridiculous that, eager as the lightning, flashed on its quarry in all things; his wit nimble and glittering as that flash, and as terrible. By the terror of his sneer he was a potentate in Europe. His epigrams pursued the prince to the recesses of his palace, and smote the general at the head of his armies, and beauty in her pride of triumph. His sarcasm hissed above the revel of saloons or the clangor of arms. "His mockery was perhaps the most terrible intellectual weapon ever wielded by man. Bigots and tyrants," says Macaulay, "who had never been moved by the wailing and cursing of millions, turned pale at his name. Principles unassailable by reason—principles that had withstood the fiercest attacks of power, the most valuable truths, the most generous sentiments, the noblest and most graceful images, the purest reputations, the most august institutions, began to look mean and loathsome, soon as that withering smile was turned upon them."

He appeared as it were the Mephistophiles of fiction, moving amid the shams, corruptions, fooleries and hypocrisies of France and Europe in the eighteenth century. In truth his genius was Satanic in its hardness and meanness, as in its brilliancy; without true sympathy with goodness or greatness. That terrible mind was the slave of puerile superstitions and petty passions, envious, malignant and egotistical. Not simply an unbeliever, his hatred to Christianity was diabolic, inexplicable except on the ground of a strange ignorance of Christianity, and a view of the deformed caricature presented in its name. His eye seems to have been blinded to all but abuses of things. He seemed to war on all that for good or evil had authority. He built no system, left no doctrine. "No human teacher ever left behind him such a wreck of truths and falsehoods." From beautiful Lake Leman he fulmined over Europe a mere genius of ruin; like Milton's archangel hurling the wrecks of the world against its author.

Close beside him in bad eminence—co-worker of ruin, history places Rousseau; similar in wondrous intellectual endowment, and united in the same evil aim; yet most unlike in genius. While Voltaire sneered away the faith of Europe, he corrupted it through the sensibilities. Its moral sense was relaxed under the fascination of his sentiment; its faith and virtue were dissolved in a paroxysm of tears. He tangled the mind of Europe with soft subtleties, dazzled it with shining sophisms, and intoxicated it with false but delicious dreams; could make Europe weep in sympathy with his romance of exquisite and heroic pathos, and admire the eloquence of his wonderful eulogy on Jesus Christ, and then could expose his illegitimate children at the doors of foundling hospitals.

The *Encyclopedists* who followed in their train, carried out to their results, and distributed throughout all the domain of science, the principles and sentiments of these master magicians. In the latter part of the reign of Louis XV., they openly aspired to effect a revolution in almost all subjects of human thought; to remold the world, its institutions, opinions and habits. The problem was to reconstruct the world and leave God out of it. The Encyclopedia—first of the name—is the monument of their combination—a work of vast service to philosophy, science, legislation and social progress; pleading for liberty against tyrannies and abuses of all kinds, but bitter with hate against Christianity belied in their presence by its professed representative. To this warfare on Christianity were marshalled the most brilliant writers of France or of Europe of that period. And what a quarry was revealed before them in a Church fatally conserving the fatuities and superstitions of twilight and spectral centuries.

For again we have to note spiritual despotism as the parent of infidelity through the *superstition* it produced. Superstition, or the irrational fear of the spiritual and unseen, naturally appears when the reason is dethroned or abandoned in the spiritual realm. But spiritual despotism in commanding belief without investigation, and in forbidding the right of private judgment, effects this dethronement and abandonment. Once allow a separation of faith from evidence, and you have made a breach in the enclosures of my creed wide enough to let in all the brood of old night and unreason; ghosts, goblins, ghouls, omens, auguries, portents, miracles, witchcrafts, visions beatific or infernal, talismanic mysteries, fatuities fantastic or satanic, without number, come trooping in, through the breach in my reason made by the intromission of wandering chapels, and transubstantiated bread and wine, and the thaumaturgic virtues of saintly rags and hair and apostolic blood and bones.

Spiritual despotism commonly enforces by direct command the reception of many superstitions; more it brings on, by the habit of mind it induces. In proof of the above statement, we have only to glance at the countries and ages of spiritual despotism. They are all overcast with phantasm and fear. But what produces superstition, produces infidelity. Their realms border on each other, there is but a step between, and the intercourse is constant. The illogical reception of a dogma prepares the way for its illogical rejection. If religion may enter without evidence, so may irreligion. As I superstitiously, that is, illogically, accept Christianity to-day, so may I with the same illogical habit admit Atheism to-morrow. Having in entering the realm of superstitious belief, renounced the light and guidance of my own reason, I am on an open, waste, dark sea, and know not on what shore I may land. The consciousness of having received a creed superstitiously will always prepare the mind to cast it away when caprice or interest prompt.

Thus superstition breaks down the barriers of rational belief in the mind. It destroys the logical law and order in the processes of the understanding; and the intellect becomes in consequence incapable of consistency or stability in its beliefs or unbeliefs. Consequently it fluctuates endlessly between childish credulity and absolute and universal unbelief.

Of this affinity or proximity between superstition and infidelity, many of the free-thinkers of the French school of the last century, and especially their great leader, Voltaire, exhibit striking instances. The men audacious as the rebel angels against the true God, cowered at a shadow. The Marquis D'Argens, one of the philosophers and courtiers of Frederick II., Macaulay describes as "hating Christianity with a rancor that made him incapable of rational inquiry, and at the same time the slave of dreams and omens, refusing to sit down to table with thirteen in company, turning pale if the salt fell toward himself, begging his guests not to cross their knives and forks on their plates, and never for the world commencing a journey on Saturday." The Marquis D'Argens is only a specimen of a class, a type of the workings of a great permanent law of mind. According to this law, we need not be surprised to find an era of skepticism bordering on that of superstition, or each becoming either, in communities or in the single mind. Still less shall we be surprised at such commingling, if we consider what effect the spectacle of superstitions enforced and warranted by the Church, and servilely received by spiritual slaves, must have had on the classes not thus receiving them—what contempt, what an indignation of unbelief such a spectacle must have provoked.

On the whole it is difficult to imagine a more terrible fountain of unbelief than that *hideous* or *ludicrous caricature, which the church of France, under the auspices of spiritual despotism, was compelled to make of Christianity before the French mind and French literati of the eighteenth century!* A religion of intellectual imbecility, ignorance and superstition, united with bigotry and arrogance, opposing itself to the enlightenment, the reason and philosophy of the age! A Church of foul and bloody history, ulcerous with lusts and corruptions, and venomous with fanaticism, affronting the moral sense of mankind and the sentiment of natural religion with the cruelties and absurdities of barbarous ages! what could be a richer quarry for the infidel wits and philosophers of that period than a church anathematizing the Baconian philosophy, warring on natural reason and the right of private judgment and execrating science! teaching transubstantiation, but ignoring Newton and La Place! and replying to all doubts and opposing utterances by acts of force and the brute thunder of ecclesiastic anathema, now contemptible from impotency, and imported from dead and barbarous eras! a Church which answered geometric demonstration or metaphysical argument with sentence of excommunication, or settled questions on natural history by scholastic formulary and pontific decretals! Could anything more surely tend to skepticism than thus arraying science against Christianity, nature against God, and human reason against revelation, which after all, reason must receive, if received at all? What could more certainly produce a sneering unbelief, than the Church assuming such a position in the presence of the encyclopedists and free-thinkers? A Church offending our natural sense of divine equity by unreasonableness in the terms and means of God's favor—securing Heaven with no purity of life through mummeries and forms and spiritual legerdemain; that attached salvation to rosaries and hair shirts! a Church which, speaking through her great Italian poet, freights the first circle of hell with "sighs which made the eternal air tremble,"

> From grief felt by multitudes many and vast,
> Of men, women and *infants that of sin*
> *Were guiltless, but for sole defect of baptism*
> Were lost!

Could such a Church be aught to them but an object of incredulous contempt? And when that Church broke a man on the wheel at Toulouse, or tortured and beheaded a youth for mere indiscretion at Abbeville, in the noon of the eighteenth century, could it be otherwise than that contempt should deepen to execration and abhorrence?

When moreover that Church came before such a tribunal as a *miracle-monger*, a *thaumaturgist* retailing monkish legends of winking statues and bleeding fountains and crucifixes fallen from Heaven, and exploits of saintly chivalry rivalling in probability and intellectual reach, if not in taste and interest, the wonderful stories of Jack the Giant Killer; tales of St. George and the Dragon, or St. Patrick and the

Serpents, or St. Anthony with fiends foul and fair, can we wonder that the world laughed outright?

But when lower still, that Church came before them as a chapman of charms and relics, showman of dry bones and old clothes, saints' tears and blood, feathers of the arch-angel Gabriel, holy coats of Christ made to pontific order, the hair and milk of the Virgin, with veils, girdles, gowns and other wardrobe enough to set up a haberdasher; heads of John the Baptist, with teeth of Peter and Paul, and apostolic legs and arms, sufficient to furnish an anatomical museum; and of wood and nails of the holy cross exhaustless in supply, can we be surprised that at the spectacle of a Church staggering down the eighteenth century under the burden of such a curiosity shop—a shout of derision went up from the philosophic corps, till Europe in sympathy shook its sides from Petersburg to the Sicilian Straits? We must recollect that by the fatal necessity of her infallibility, that Church could renounce nothing, repent nothing, amend nothing. With all the trumpery and pretension, and absurdity of the past cumbered and bedizzened, not a shred bleached, or a stain removed from her robes that had trailed through the foulness and bloodshed of a thousand years, she was pinioned and pilloried to the derision of all time. Fatal was the hour for Rome when she put forth the claim to be the Infallible. The infallible is the immutable.

All retreat was closed up. Each step in her usurpation was upon the round of a ladder that broke as she rose. There is for her no descent but in a fall that must dash her in pieces. Still, descend she must. It were terrible for any institution to be compelled to go down all the future bearing the burden of all the past. It would crush it as under the pressure of fate. How then could the Gallic church go down through the searching and fiery ordeal of the eighteenth century without being burned up. But this Church was to the French nation at large, and to the peoples of central and southern Europe, yea even to the philosophers, their all of Christianity. They hardly knew any other. With such a representative of Christianity, encountering such a literary cohort as the philosophers and the encyclopedists, is it strange that in the heart of the French nation there sprang up a pest of unbelief destined to waste the world?

There seemed to be wanting, in order to complete the odiousness and defencelessness of the French church, only *the historical and logical exposé, and the fall, during the period, of the Order of Jesus;* the latter stripping her of her most powerful defenders, after the former had drawn on her the hatred of mankind for crimes even beyond her own guilt and turpitude. Indeed through the creation and employment of this order as its instrument and champion, spiritual despotism may be rightly arraigned as being to a fearful extent the guilty cause of the revolt of the human mind from Christianity in the eighteenth century. Jesuitism, as far as it stands before mankind as the representative and champion of Christianity, must evidently have brought on our religion odium and incredulity, by its utter immorality in theory, policy and practice, whenever its creed and conduct became known. No institution known to history has been more daringly, more corruptingly or more impiously immoral; its creed, a gospel of deceit; its principia a novum organum of craft—the dialectic of fraud; its chief virtue and piety, submission absolute to spiritual despotism. In its policy and conduct, it scrupled in compassing its ends no shape, garb or hue, no art, no measure. It wore the livery of all schools; humored all caprices, moods, temperaments, opinions and passions; passed from virtue to vice and from heroism to meanness with most absolute indifferency; made the end sanctify all means and canonize all crimes. Its protean facility of change and flexibility of principle was portentous. It could cabal in the name of all creeds, political and social; could personate all characters; could enact the absolutist or the servile; the anchorite or the courtier and gallant; the lewd and blasphemous wit, or the austere devotee and rapt enthusiast. Democrat, aristocrat and monarchist; the instrument, ally, slave of despotism or the red republican; a sower of rumors, conspirator against monarchy, and assassin of kings—in all these parts and persons, with equal facility to suit place, and time, and circle, and country, it passed before the eyes of men.

Of course such an utter recklessness of principle, assuming the championship of Christianity, and sanctioned and canonized by the power claiming to be its infallible and Heaven-appointed hierophant on earth—such a recklessness and profligacy of principle, we say, thus assuming and thus sanctioned in the name of Religion, must—as far as those assumptions and sanctions are admitted—destroy either the religious faith or the moral sense of mankind. Religion thus presented shocks the natural conscience. The former cannot find place in the human bosom till it has expelled the latter.

Such is ever the curse of spiritual despotism. Through the instruments it is compelled to employ, it is necessitated to smite nations with a moral plague or with infidelity; fills them with moral banditti or spiritual slaves; and establishes its throne only over the sepulchre of the conscience or the smothered crater of volcanic unbelief. An instrument necessitating such consequences to the French church and the Romish world, in the seventeenth and eighteenth centuries, was Jesuitism. And its mischiefs were likely to be *extensive and terrible in proportion to the extent of its sphere and its power*. But in the ages previous, the Order of Jesus had possessed itself of all the strongholds which command the public mind. The pulpit, press, confessional and inquisition, and the academy and university through Catholic Europe, belonged to it. Cabinet and Cathedral were extensively occupied by it. Literature and science were its creatures or its wards. In colonial adventure and missions, in politics, in finance, wars, treaties, tariffs, trade and manufactures; in short, in almost every interest of society the Jesuit figured. In Austria he was confessor and master of the bigot Ferdinand II., and abettor of the thirty years' war; in France the assassin of Henry IV., keeper of conscience to Charles IX. and Louis XIV., instigator of the massacre of St. Bartholomew and the revocation of the edict of Nantes; in Spain he was the evil genius of Phillip II.; in Holland the murderer of the Duke of Orange; in England the complotter of midnight cabal, and regicide conspiracy. The meshes of the policy of the order were all over Europe, and in distant continents. Through its subtle, quick and all-pervading system of intelligence, it had a constant, universal, instantaneous consciousness of the world. Through its centralized administration, its absolute autocracy and its mechanic obedience, it momently penetrated with one adamantine, remorseless, ruthless will its vast domain from Central Europe to China and California. Its ear and whisper, its eye and hand were everywhere; everywhere, its intrigue and police, its poison and stiletto. It was to Christendom a terrible power; but one which, like the old man of the sea, could not be shaken off. Odious everywhere through its cabal and its crimes, feared everywhere because of its vast, insidious, unprincipled ambition and influence, aspiring to grasp all interests from fashion to finance, proscribed at times, in disgust and exhaustion of endurance, from almost every court and country in Europe—it had again been recalled as the necessary instrument of the papal and royal despotism of the period we treat of. At length in its feud with the Jansenists, it committed the offence unpardonable in Parisian eyes, of showing itself ridiculous as well as tyrannical and unprincipled. Through his inimitable provincial letters, Pascal made France and all Europe laugh at it. The order, too mighty for popes and potentates, was impaled on his satire. Finally, when its seals of secrecy were broken by a judicial procedure and its books by compulsory process were brought before the legal tribunal, in a trial where the Jesuits as a mercantile company were a party, the exposure of its esoteric creed and rules of practice drew on it the abhorrence of Christendom. The moral legerdemain therein displayed, the subtle glazing of sin, the saturnine coolness of its atrocious sophisms, the impudent naïveté of its infernal dialectic, divided Christendom between a shudder and sneer. Jesuitism shrank before the tempest of odium and ridicule aroused against it, and for a time disappears before the indignation of mankind. But as by its policy and achievement in behalf of spiritual despotism, it had shaken the faith of nations in Christianity; so now by its fall stripping spiritual despotism of its right arm of spiritual fraud, and bereaving it of its most efficient defenders, it broke the strength of that tyranny which had essayed thus far to extort a nominal confession of Christianity from the ghastly and anguish-wreathed lips of crushed nations. Its fall broke the seals of the pit its triumph had peopled. The agency of the Jesuits as nominal champions of Christianity, associating it with their infamies, was undoubtedly one reason for that fierce rage with which the nations came to regard the religion of Christ. The recoil of an agency so utterly unprincipled and profligate, when exposed, must have been terrible against the power that employed it, *i. e.* against the Romish church; and in the nations where she alone represented Christianity, against religion itself. The shock to faith must have been the more fatal, the more intimately and pervasively Jesuitism had intertwined itself with the political and social order of the world, and had poisoned its moral life. So wide-spread was the cancerous growth, that we need not wonder its attempted eradication almost cost the spiritual life of Christendom.

We may not close this view of the rise of infidelity in France, and its diffusion from her through the rest of Europe, without adding to all the above causes, tending to make her during the eighteenth century the hot-bed of unbelief, *the unparalleled prevalence there of the money madness of the era.* In France was its especial focus, or at least, owing to peculiar qualities of the French character, it had like almost all the passions of modern civilization, its acme of fever at Paris. The illusions, frauds, corruptions and crimes attendant upon it, there were stupendous. Like all the vices and follies of the French character, it seems to have come to its height under the infamous Regent of Orleans. Nor can we wonder that the national mind already alien or indifferent to religion, from many causes, should have been well-nigh borne clear away when this storm of Mammonism beat upon it. The world of faith faded. The world of sight closed around and snared them in the meanest, most sordid, materializing of the passions. The class of infidel economists which arose and applied the energy of brilliant, sagacious, godless genius to the science of wealth, fitly illustrate the spirit of the period. The spiritual power—the Church—which should have stayed the plague, rather aggravated it. She even led the way, into the temple of Mammon. The position and history of France illustrate the terrible mischiefs which must accrue when the spiritual power abandons its functions of checking the material and secular tendencies of modern civilization.

But if we attempt to trace the money plague to its source, we track its malignancy at last to the same evil fountain which we have found gushing forth with skepticism in forms and directions so manifold over Christendom. The ultimate guilt of this plague lies with spiritual despotism. Not that she was answerable for that stage of civilization and social and historical development that of necessity lifted the idea of wealth to a new prominence before the mind of society. That stage was inevitable; nay more, was desirable. It was in the line of social progress. That wealth should rise to a high and commanding interest amid the forces and objects of society, was natural; was beneficent. But that it should become an epidemic mania, a moral plague, corrupting the faith and life of nations, was due to the fact that spiritual despotism had broken the moral constitution of the world, had slain or enfeebled faith, exhausted the energies of the religious sentiment by ages of agony and blood, and had left the world with no conservative or recuperative power to withstand the invasions of any epidemic moral disorder. Otherwise, like the nutriment that in the weak produces fevers, while to the strong it gives strength, the money interest and passion of the era in question, might have blent healthfully and beneficently with the life and forces of modern society.

Thus through influences such as we have enumerated, have we seen France becoming amid the nations of Europe the great elaborator and diffuser of infidelity. Here was its geographic centre and capital. Here its chief theatre. Here its mightiest tragedy; its most brilliant and most atrocious exploits; and here its earth-shaking catastrophe. And from hence, also, as from its Jerusalem, the gospel of unbelief went forth to dazzle and to darken nations. Such an elaborator and diffuser, France became, if we seek its chief, primary and ultimate cause, in consequence of the *politico-ecclesiastical despotism applied for centuries to the French mind*—applied with force not enough to smother, but only to render its action within its more confined space more intense, passionate and explosive; force driving it from affairs to the discussion and resolution of first principles and the achievement of results in primary philosophy, that like the analysis of reputed elementary substances in chemistry, seemed capable of accomplishment only under great pressure.

In a national mind thus coerced into revolutionary ways in philosophy, and emerging, wearied, exhausted and disgusted from generations of religious wars into which the same despotism had impelled it, we have seen the same evil cause again generating infidelity by enfeebling and corrupting the spiritual power; making it incompetent to resist the invasions of the money-plague or any moral epidemic; betraying it into enormous and suicidal crimes; making it the slave or showman of debasing and puerile superstitions; associating with it as champion and instrument, an order the most profligate and odious in Christendom; and presenting it as accomplice of the Valois and the Bourbons in their unspeakable sins and shames, and their conspiracies against the liberties of the nation.

We have seen the spiritual power under the coercion of spiritual despotism, made to enact this part in French history in the presence of such an amphitheatre of mind as the world had never seen before, so witty and so wicked, so unprincipled and so audacious, so terrible in its sneer, so keen in its sense of the ridiculous, so brilliant and rapid in its apprehension, so daring and irreverent in its analysis.

We have seen this amphitheatre of the French mind in view of such a spectacle of ecclesiastic history passing before it, filling all Europe with its hiss and derision, and ultimately organizing the erudition, science, fancy, wit and eloquence, most eminent in Europe, into a conspiracy against Christianity; and then we have seen this moving forth from Paris as a centre, with a cohort of disciples, confessors, evangelists and apostles, gifted, powerful, Heaven-defiant and Heaven-hating—with the enthusiasm of a new dispensation and the zeal of new love and new wrath—towards the overthrow of the "reign of superstition" the world over. We find the diffusion of this plague of skepticism from France over Europe powerfully aided, moreover, by the central and commanding position of France in European Civilization, presenting her monarchy, court, literature and manners as the model and law for Christendom, and tending to make ideas which had become French, become ultimately European.

Such in general was the agency of France in producing that eclipse of faith we are investigating. Through all influences and causes, permeating like the pulse of an evil heart the entire system, giving virulent malignant life to all, we find spiritual despotism.

CHAPTER IX.

SPIRITUAL DESPOTISM IN ITALY AND SPAIN.

ITALY.—Spiritual Despotism a generator of Infidelity in Italy and Spain—Italian History mutilated and stifled—Its silence significant —Insurrection of Mind indicated by the measures of Repression— Their Multitude and Atrocity—Censorships—Proscriptions—Crusades—Massacres—Dominicans—Franciscans—The Inquisition— Glimpses of Infidelity in Italian History and Literature—Infidelity a necessity of Pontifical History applied to the Italian mind—The Troubadour—Dante—Petrarch—Arnold of Brescia—Savonarola— Infidel Scholars—Monarchs—Popes—Repressive measures of the Sixteenth Century—Their utter mercilessness—Terror—Silence —Italy stifled but not believing.

SPAIN.—Orthodoxy of Spain—No Spasm in a Corpse—The Inquisition, the instrument of Spanish Faith—Its mystery and terror— War on Books—Index Expurgatorus—Death struggle of the Spanish mind, 1559-1570—Spanish Thought, Literature, Civilization, Manhood fall together—Silence not belief—The Peninsula still seething with insurgent Infidelity—Three Realms of Spiritual Despotism compared.

CONCLUSION.

Résumé of the Argument—Lessons for the Times—Doom of Spiritual Despotism.

BEFORE closing our review of the phenomenon under discussion, in order to the completeness of our argument of the question of cause as between spiritual liberty and spiritual despotism, or between Protestantism and Romanism, *it is requisite to take a brief glance at those countries of Europe which might seem to contradict our conclusions*, and at which spiritual despotism sometimes points as monuments of her conservative power against unbelief—SPAIN and ITALY. "In Italy and Spain," we are told, "as also in Austria and other Catholic countries of Europe, spiritual despotism prevailed. But behold the exemplary and submissive faith of Spain. Why this? and why the quiet and steadfastness of the Italian mind? Behold here the triumph of the Catholic communion, the peace and unity and endurance in believing, which it ensures! why, if spiritual despotism be the mother of infidelity, why did she not produce that offspring in the two Peninsulas as well as in France?" To these inquiries we answer:

First, spiritual despotism alone, without the requisite concomitancy, of course will not assure the result. It is so with all causes. Their environment is an essential part of them. Despotism that absolutely stifles thought or expression will not be likely to breed a clamorous infidelity. The dead will not catch the plague. The malaria will breed no fever in a corpse. Yet the plague is contagious, and the malaria a poisoner. Our reasonings of the effect of spiritual despotism, of course imply a *living subject.* We expect not madness or spasm in the slain.

Secondly, we maintain that spiritual despotism *did produce its legitimate consequences in those countries*, and if skepticism was not as *apparent* in their history as in that of France, its suppression accomplished by the means it has been, is easily explicable, consistently with our main proposition, and has cost those countries evils, compared with which even the rampant infidelity of France were a lighter curse.

First, then, we charge that spiritual despotism did produce its natural evil fruit of unbelief in those countries. In proof, look we first at Italy. There it produced it even earlier; inasmuch as society there in all its developments matured earlier, and Rome the great capital and centre of spiritual despotism, was nearer; in consequence some of its natural results were more immediately exhibited.

It is with a feeling of profound melancholy we pursue this argument through Italian history. That history is to us ineffably sad, not so much because of its utterances as its silence. That it speaks so timidly, so meagrely, so brokenly, on facts so many, so patent and so vast as those embraced in the insurrectionary movements of the Italian mind against the Christian faith, or at least against the Church; its dumbness, or speaking below its breath on topics of such tragic and commanding interest, is among the most affecting and instructive of the facts it exhibits. That we have to catch at implication, allusion, obscure hints, scattered and isolate events, sketches, glimpses, fragmentary narratives, for proof of facts which, if real, ought to have been chronicled with trumpet tongue, and with accuracy and fullness of blazon for all time, is in itself the strongest of the proofs we seek. That we are compelled to eke out evidence from coherent or causative facts, from unguarded outflashings of sentiment or passion in the narrator, from the figure of the poet, the sneer of the satirist, the epigram of the wit, is painfully significant. Such silence has a terrible eloquence. That historic record, torn, mutilated, bleared and blotted all over with tears and blood, what language can speak so much. We seem to be listening to the broken sobs and hushed breathings of a crushed, writhing and stifled victim, exhausted with agony and terror. Could any description so prove the guilt of the "great quell?" the deadly wrong wrought to the mind of Italy? Ages of spiritual tyranny, espionage, intimidation and bloody repression look out on us from that marred and stifled record. That noble and gifted Italian mind—for centuries it must have been beaten down, awed, gagged and all but suffocated through all that glorious peninsula. How terrible and ruthless must have been the pressure of tyranny to have accomplished such a result!

We may measure the strength of an upheaving, by the force requisite to keep it down. So we may estimate the insurrectionary movement of the Italian mind against spiritual despotism, by the frightful measures of repression employed. Thus the ruthless policy of potentates and hierarchs, the introduction of the Inquisition into Italy, the institution of the gloomy orders of the Dominicans and Franciscans, (minions of repression), censorships, sanguinary edicts, proscriptions, imprisonment, exile, murder, massacre, to what a strength of revolt in the mind of Italy, were such appliances addressed? yea, each martyr flame, the axe, the dungeon, the Holy Office, they have each a terrible significance. All point to spiritual despotism fastening on beautiful, glorious Italy, aiming to strangle its soul. We see the weird and talon fingers on the throat of the victim; we hear the death rattle; and that is all! Such is the impression on us of the testimony of Italian literature on our present question.

From causes and facts of which we have indubitable knowledge, we are certified of a formidable reaction against the spiritual power in Italy, as inevitable. That that reaction took its course toward infidelity, we also know, not only from the laws of mind acting in the circumstances, but also from a great variety of historic testimony, specific or by way of direct implication or allusion. Evidence of it glimpses upon us also, whenever the literature of the drama, the romance, the ballad or satire, or that of homiletics, politics, judicature or philosophy, lift for a moment the veil from the muffled national mind. There is a current strong and distinct as of the rapids above the cataract. It is as though we stood near the brink of an abyss, and saw multitudes borne continually towards its verge; and then disappearing. We need no description or narrative to tell us what waits beyond. A broken shriek, a mighty groan caught by snatches wailing up from the darkness, is enough. We know death is below. Such is the evidence for the most part, that comes to us of infidelity in Italy produced by spiritual despotism. We see multitudes borne along the dark stream, impelled by forces they are ill able to resist, to the verge of that fatal steep of skepticism from which, alas! few of the sons of genius ever return. There they disappear. They pass into the gloom and silence of a system of despotic ruthless repression, that lets in no light on its victims, and allows no ear to listen too nearly to their stifled curse and groan. A deep wail, a vast sigh, a death-shriek breaking up at intervals from the darkness and silence, fills up the chapter. But we need no more. The terrible reactive force toward unbelief caused by spiritual despotism is abundantly proved in Italy, though most of its utterances have been foully and bloodily smothered.

That infidelity should spring up under the shadow of such thrones as during the mediæval era claimed to be the seat of God's vicegerent on earth, as naturally as the poisonous mushroom and night-shade in the mephitic damp and dark, there needs neither history nor prophecy to certify us. Popes foul with almost all crimes of human nature and those beyond it, passing before such a mind as that of Italy in the middle ages and those immediately subsequent, men lifted to the pontifical chair by the bribery and violence of bandit nobles, or the favors of frail ladies of the Roman patricianate, or by ecclesiastic intrigue, conspiracy and simony bidding for the spiritual empire of mankind; men dragging along their imperial purple and scarlet smeared with rapine, incest and murder—from the vision of such men as vicegerents of God, the covert of hideous atheism itself were a refuge! Monsters like Cæsar Borgia and Alexander V., literary sybarites or paganized amateurs and dilettanti, like the Sextuses and Leos; the gloomy fanatacism of the Innocents; the ferocious bigotry of the Pauls and Victors, the lust and gluttony and homicide of the Benedicts and Johns; and the political ambition and cabal of the Bonifaces,

Clements and Gregories—these and such a lineage as to a great extent for ages seized the sceptre of St. Peter—a lineage where the miser and intriguant, the debauchee, the fanatic and the assassin, oft succeed each other, oft seem blent in infernal perfectness of sin in the same person—such a dynasty sitting in the seat of God, the infallible expositors and oracles of the divine word, having the lordship of faith and morals and the keys of Heaven—such a dynasty of a kingdom of truth and love, with the crucified Galilean for its founder and the sermon on the Mount for its fundamental law! such men in such a position! it were enough to send a tremor of horror or laughter through the whole earth. A solecism so blasphemous were enough to draw on it at once the bolts of outraged heaven and the blasts of a world's sneer and hate.

And when we learn that the *lower orders of the hierarchy and the regular and secular clergy were to a melancholy degree, to such a pontificate, "fit body to fit head;"* when we look at the *surroundings* of the pontificate, its court thronged with men steeped through and through with the filth and fraud and blood of Italian politics in the middle ages, or its environment with groups ecclesiastical, political or literary, which seemed to make Papal, like Pagan Rome, in its origin, a city of refuge among the nations, and to convert the Lateran conclave into a focus of Machiavellian cabal and conspiracy for all Europe—it seems like one of the pictures the daring muse of Dante has hung on the walls of Eternal Night; it grows on the vision like the palace of infernal Dis amid its setting of ninefold Hells.

With such a spectacle before the Italian mind, arrogating to be the high court of Jesus Christ on earth, intervening between the visions of the million and the Redeemer, and with bloody and blinding enforcement compelling the acceptance of itself by them, as the representative of Christianity, what else could have resulted than a shudder of unbelief through the peninsula? "If such," (men must have reasoned) "if such are God's vicegerents, who then are Satan's? such the holders of heaven's keys; who then shall stand at the doors of hell?"

With such necessary induction from known historic facts and laws of the human mind, we can translate utterances and facts, which Italian history and literature, spite of inquisition and censorship, have at times allowed to escape them, significant of a strong, deep undercurrent of skepticism in the popular mind, flowing beneath mute or servile ages. We read in them the indubitable signs of a vast defection from the Christian faith. With such guides to interpretation, we recognize in the jest of the *Troubadour*, already in the twelfth century, the sneer of the philosopher of the eighteenth. In the sarcasm of Raymond De Castelnau, "if God saves those whose sole merit consists in loving good living, and handsome women; if friars the black and white, and templars and hospitallers win the joys of paradise, great fools in sooth were St. Andrew and St. Peter, who suffered so much for what these men win so easily;" in such utterances, flinging out from time to time in literature, we have assurances that the atrocious solecism of a religion without morality, was producing its natural effect of derision and incredulity, toward its professed representatives, likely to be directed ultimately against the faith itself thus caricatured and belied.

Amid the multitudinous testimony furnished by Italian literature, turn we a moment to their great *national poets*, to the poets rather than the philosophers or even historians, because they more livingly and with less effective repression of the censor, reflect the national feeling. Glance a moment at the great Homeric oracles of the genius of Italy in the middle ages, Dante and Petrarch. Was not spiritual despotism producing a revolt of the Italian mind from the papal church, a revolt of necessity ultimating in infidelity, to a people shut out from all other representation of Christianity—when Dante, in his wondrous vision, places some of the highest dignitaries of that Church amid reprobates in hell? and describes Rome as the Babylon of revelations? How far from skepticism was the Italian mind, when looking forth on the papacy as representing Christianity, it utters itself in the Divine Comedia; which poem, in its nineteenth canto exhibits Pope Nicholas III. in one of the circles of inferno, suspended with head downward through certain apertures in the burning rock, with legs projecting upward and blazing like a lamp, and, in this most unpontifical posture, awaiting the coming of worse miscreants than himself, Clement V. and Boniface VIII. How far from infidelity must that mind be that drew that picture, so far as popedom, that is, spiritual despotism concreted in the Romish See, was Christianity. How far again from unbelief was the same Italian mind, thus expressing itself in another passage in that same poem, in apostrophe to the papacy:

"Your avarice
Overcasts the world with mourning, under foot
Treading the good and raising bad men up.
Of Shepherds like to you, the Evangelist
Was ware, when her who sits upon the waves
With kings in filthy whoredom, he beheld;
She who with seven heads towered at her birth,
And from ten horns her proof of glory drew.
Of gold and silver ye have made your God, &c."

Proof ample this, of ecclesiastical corruption bred of spiritual despotism, and sure to breed infidelity, if not, of infidelity itself.

Was Italy of unruffled faith, again, when even the mild Petrarch, member of the ecclesiastical body and favored resident of the papal court, spite of ambition, interest, love and gratitude, fled the Roman court as the spot where he saw crimes of religious usurpation heightened by the "abandonment of every virtue?" and when from his retirement in Vaucluse he thus raised his revered and dreaded voice against the corruptions of Rome?

"From impious Babylon—from whence
All shame hath fled and every good is gone:
Mother of errors—dwelling-place of grief
I've fled!
May flames from Heaven upon their tresses fall;
O forge of treachery! O prison dire!
Death-place of every virtue, nurse of every ill,
Hell of the living! great the miracle
If Christ rouse not at length his tardy ire!
Unblushing wretch! what hope remains for thee?"

These are signs—signs if not of absolute skepticism, of minds verging toward it, and of the presence of ecclesiastical corruption—the foul birth of spiritual despotism—sure to produce it.

With signs such as these, selected from poets that

were good churchmen and national oracles in the Italian literature of the fourteenth and fifteenth centuries, we are not surprised to find that Luther in his visit to Rome, in the sixteenth century, was shocked at hearing expressions of a flippant and sneering skepticism from beside the altar and under the very shadows of the Vatican.

With the above causes, in the ecclesiastic condition and constitution of Italy, and the tendencies of the Italian mind exhibited in its literature, correspond other *facts presented in its general history*, in fragmentary form and without logical relation, but showing evidence of the same movement toward religious revolt and skepticism in the Italian mind—such facts as these for instance; that for ages one half of Italy were in open and direct warfare with the papacy; that not only dukes, princes and military chiefs, but entire principalities and the common people of the cities, defied fearlessly the authority of the supreme spiritual lord of Christendom and the terrors of the interdicts and excommunication; that in the chronicles of the different republics and the lives of the most distinguished Italians for ages—statesmen, publicists, poets, and philosophers—we meet with a constant vein of hostility to the professed Head of the Church. Such facts stand before us as natural consequences of disastrous causes already considered, and significant of a profound revolt against the spiritual power; a revolt which inevitably, in the absence of a knowledge of true Christianity tyrannously hid from Italy by this power, must have become revolt against Christianity itself. The appearance also of such men as Arnold of Brescia in the twelfth, and a Savonarola in the fifteenth century, and such facts as the founding of the Franciscan and Dominican orders in the twelfth century, as champions and bulwarks of the Romish church against perceived dangers, and antagonist to the mental activity and growing intelligence manifested in the Paterini and Albigenses, are exponents of the same great movement in the Italian mind. When we are told, as we are by Sismondi in his history of Italy (page 70) of Frederic II. the most brilliant of the Hohenstaufens, that while he loved literature and encouraged learning, founding schools and universities, and was distinguished for an intellectual suppleness, a taste for philosophy, and a great independence of opinion, he manifested also a leaning toward infidelity—when we are told again by the same author that in Italy, subsequently and especially after the translation of the books of Averrhoes, "thinkers throughout Italy were accused by priests not only of heresy but of Epicurism and infidelity," and "the young men of the court of the

De Medici, devoted to ancient literature, were charged with preferring the religion of the ancient Romans to that of the Church"—when such statements are presented they do not surprise us. Such combination of unbelief with intelligence we should regard as inevitable in the circumstances of Italian history in that period.

So, again, when a reliable historic writer states (Green's Historic studies) that with men of brightest intellect in Italy in the sixteenth century, religious investigation terminated in skepticism; and that notoriously in the epoch of Luther, "not only the universities of Italy but also the churches were filled with men whose brilliant talents and profound learning had not sufficed to save them from infidelity"—such a statement exhibits to us only a natural and logical sequence of causes already known, springing from the spiritual despotism and ecclesiastic constitution and condition of Italy. It was a necessary result, verified by the logic as well as record of history, that Italy should be, as it notoriously was in the sixteenth century, full of unbelievers—infidel princes, courtiers, statesmen, captains, artists, writers; indeed *infidel monks, priests, bishops, cardinals*, turn up everywhere. Yea in the person of Leo X., as in some popes before and after him, infidelity seems to have sat on the throne of the Romish world. Infidelity thus took up its abode in monastery, cathedral, sacristy and oratory, behind the chancel, yea even beneath the triple crown itself.

Thus down into the sixteenth century, despotism had borne its grapes of Sodom. Rome was startled in the early part of that century, not by the unbelief that spread through her like a pontine miasm, but by *finding a faith springing up that dared to see a God and believe in a Christ apart from herself.* Protestantism at length alarmed her, whom atheism only lulled to a voluptuous repose. She took measures ruthless, awfully summary. She roused from her soft dream of sensual and intellectual voluptuousness, her engrossment with "choice cookery, delicious wines, lovely women, hounds, falcons, horses, newly discovered manuscripts of the classics, sonnets and burlesque romances in the sweetest Tuscan just as licentious as a pure sense of the graceful would permit"—from these she roused herself to a banquet of blood, the noblest blood of Italy. She called in the Inquisition; and clothed it with powers and infused into it a spirit that made it a whisper of horror from Calabria to the Alps. Its adamantine mercilessness and its impartial cruelties seemed borrowed of the king of Hell. No rank nor wealth, nor privilege of republics, nor favor of kings, was a safeguard. The timid convert and the enthusiastic proselyte were alike exposed to accusation. Cassock and cowl were no longer a protection; monks were drawn forth from the secrecy of the cloister; the learned from the seclusion of their studies; the sanctities of domestic life were violated; superstition and fear were everywhere. The stake, the robe of pitch, the knife, the axe, the rack, the hunt of heretics through the forest and the high Alps, the martyrdoms of famine and flight, of the desolate cave, the subterranean dungeon and of the midnight Adriatic—these with infernal energy consummated the work. A deep, voiceless, almost breathless terror pervaded Italy. The mind of Italy was strangled in her gore.

But this silence was not *belief*. Did Italy though crushed and strangled, *believe* the grisly horror standing on her breast, with the sword to her throat, and calling itself Christianity—did she believe that ogre to be a God? From such a religion she would hide behind eternal night. No! underneath Italy now lies an infidelity deep though silent, as her earthquake, till her hour is come, and then destined to be as terrible. No; Italy is no exception to our general argument; spiritual despotism did breed skepticism, she quenched Protestantism but could not restore faith. Superstition and infidelity now divide the Peninsula—twin curses—almost making the emancipation of Italy a despair.

SPAIN.

Such is the vaunted repose of faith spiritual despotism has secured to Italy. Let us now turn a moment and glance at that other country in Europe, often appealed to as a monument of the power of spirtual despotism to save nations from infidelity. Why, it may be asked, did not Spain exhibit the same passionate insurrection against Christianity as the neighboring peoples of Europe during the eighteenth century? We answer as in case of Italy, for the same reason that the blinded see no startling sights; that a man in chains and prison is guilty of no highway robbery; that a corpse is not troubled with convulsion and fever. Spiritual despotism excluded infidelity as the grave shuts out delirium. The secret of this exclusion, the instrument alike of Spanish and of Italian orthodoxy is found in one word—that word, the ultimate logic of spiritual despotism—a word most hateful, hideous, accursed in the vocabulary of modern history—the inquisition; the panacea for heresy that cures by killing. *It suppressed infidelity by stifling the Spanish mind.* Whenever that mind has revived, on the removal of the suffocating pressure of the holy office, unbelief, as in the last age, immediately sprang up again. In the era of the French Revolution infidelity crossed the Pyrenees before the columns of Napoleon.

This terrible engine for crushing the minds of nations, the inquisition, was, strange to relate, introduced into Spain by the heroic and gentle Isabella in 1481. It was probably the most frightful and effective instrument of intellectual repression ever invented by man. In the first year of its existence, in the single province of Andalusia alone, it burned two thousand victims, in addition to seventeen thousand who suffered a less severe punishment than the stake. "All its action," says Ticknor, "was in secrecy and in darkness. From the moment when the inquisition laid its grasp on the object of its suspicions, no voice was heard to issue from its cells. Often the victim was never after heard of. He disappeared from men. Men's minds were appalled. Imagination was filled with horror at the idea of a power so vast, so silent, so omnipresent, and which killed by a blow from out an impenetrable gloom. Soon its warfare was turned against the thoughts of men, even more than their external crimes. The intellectual and cultivated peculiarly felt the sense of personal security more and more shaken. They resisted only to perish."

Its next step was a *war on books.* When the Lutheran reform broke out, and seemed to threaten Spain, 1521, then fulminated forth from Rome *the edict against Spanish thought*; war especially was declared against Lutheran books. The Grand Inquisition immediately issued orders for search and seizure of all heretical books. Already, in 1496, the inquisition under Torquemada had burned large quantities of Hebrew bibles, and other manuscripts at Seville, as Jewish writings. It now claimed the right of examining all books and determining what might be published. In 1526, was published in Spain the first *Index Expurgatorius*, with denunciation by Philip II. of confiscation and death against any person who should sell, or buy, or keep in possession, any book prohibited by that index. There was now a direct death-grapple with the intellectual life of Spain. It was as though the horrid instrument of torture, called the "Maiden," invented and applied by the inquisition to the bodies of men, was with the embrace of its arms of steel and its dagger-fingers, applied to the Spanish soul. Such was the infernal pitilessness with which the murder of the Spanish mind was prosecuted. The contest was terrible, but brief. In ten years, from 1559 to 1570, Protestanism was smothered in its own blood throughout the Spanish peninsula. Minds the noblest and loftiest in it, perished, and elements that might have saved Spain ages of superstition, and irreligion, and shame, were eliminated from the Spanish civilization. By a brief of Pope Paul IV.,

1558, the inquisition was required to proceed *against all suspected persons*, be they bishops, archbishops, cardinals, dukes, kings, or emperors; a power the most terrible ever created against progress, in the history of mankind. The auto da fè, followed at Valladolid and elsewhere. "The number of victims was not large compared with earlier periods; seldom more than twenty being burned at once." "But among these were the leading active minds of the age." "Men of learning," says Ticknor, "were peculiarly obnoxious to suspicion, since the cause of Protestantism appealed directly to learning for its support. Sanchez, the best classical scholar of his time in Spain, Louis de Leon, the best Hebrew critic and most eloquent preacher, and Miranda, the chief Spanish historian, with other men of letters, were summoned before the inquisition. No rank or position, or holiness, or circumstances of life, exempted from mistrust, if they but showed a tendency to inquiry." Thus was the deadliest and guiltiest of crimes man can commit attempted on Spain, the massacre of its intelligence, reason and thought. The great purpose of spiritual despotism was in ten years accomplished, at least further than in any other Christian country before or since.

The policy of repression and expulsion of religious dissent, was followed up with atrocious ruthlessness.

The tiger-appetite of fanatacism roused in the infernal game, was never allowed to slacken. The expulsion of six hundred thousand Moors, the most peaceable and industrious of Spanish subjects, is merely one of its waymarks. *Spanish manhood* perished under its dreadful pressure. Soon all writers and books show marks of utter intellectual subjugation. "From the abject title pages and 'dedications,'" says Ticknor, "of the authors themselves, through crowds of certificates collected from friends, to establish the orthodoxy of works as little connected with religion as fairy tales, down to the colophon supplicating pardon for any unconscious neglect of the authority of the Church, or any too *free use of classical mythology*, we are continually oppressed with painful proofs, how completely the human mind was enslaved in Spain." The natural consequences ensued. Life and power, with freedom, soon passed from the Spanish character. With its loyalty and dignity, its earnest faith likewise perished. Spain shrivelled and wasted as by a slow plague; from the position of the proudest and noblest nation in Europe, threatening the earth with universal empire, she sank, almost within a single life of man, to feebleness, servility, and almost to utter dissolution. No nation in Christendom had fallen from such a height of power to such an abyss of degradation. Spiritual despotism had struck her from her very "pride of place," down for ever; and applied to her the vampire embrace of the inquisition, till she lay prostrate, bloodless, faint and dying, her breath of agony hushed under a vast fear. Intellectual independence and manly freedom, were crushed, chained, and starved to death. The commonest forms of truth were excluded; the human mind pined and dwarfed for want of nourishment. The great sciences, both moral and physical, that for a century had been illumining and quickening the rest of Europe, were unable to force their way through "the jealous guard, which ecclesiastical and political despotism had joined, to keep for ever watching at the gates of the Pyrenees." All instruction not approved by the Church, was treated as dangerous. At the university no elegant learning was fostered, save such as was fitted to form scholastic churchmen and faithful Catholics. The physical and exact sciences were carefully forbidden, except so far as they could be taught on the authority of Aristotle. The scholastic philosophy continued to be regarded as the highest form of intellectual culture. Diego de Torres tells us, it was by mere accident, after having been five years at the university of Salamanca, the first in the kingdom, that he learned even the existence of the mathematical sciences. The common forms of knowledge, were to an incredible extent kept out of the country. On the other hand, errors, follies, absurdities, sprang up and abounded. Astrology, celestial portents, and disastrous influences of comets, were universal superstitions in Spain, in the beginning of the eighteenth century; while the system of Copernicus was forbidden to be taught as contrary to the scriptures; and the philosophy of Bacon, with all its fruits was "unknown."

Even as late as 1785, Ensenuado as minister of State made report to Charles the VII., as follows, "There is not a *professorship of public law or of experimental science, or of Anatomy or of Botany in the kingdom!* We have *no exact Geographical maps of the country* (in 1785!!) or of its provinces, nor anybody who can make them, so that we depend on France and Holland, and are shamefully ignorant of the true relations and distances of our own towns." So in 1771 Salamanca answered to Charles VII. urging the universities to change their ancient habits, and teach the physical and exact sciences, "Newton teaches nothing that would make a good logician or metaphysician, and Gossendi and Des Cartes do not agree so well with revealed truth as Aristotle does."

But enough, we see what the boasted exemption of Spain from infidelity amounted to, and what it has cost, and how it was effected. It has cost the intellectual and moral life, the enlightenment, the dignity, and "*earnest faith*" of the Spanish mind; and to the nation, its greatness and glory of character and empire. Its fruits are still discernible not only in decrepid, prostrate, distracted, impoverished, dark-minded Spain, with the fanaticism and crime of its millions, and the indescribable corruption and imbecility of its court; but in the vast and magnificent climes of this continent, over which the shadow of her empire and soul have fallen like the wing of the dark angel. Nor has this suicidal policy saved her even from unbelief. It *must* have generated it deep in the soul of Spain. Signs unmistakable manifested themselves in the era of the French revolution in spite of the inquisition; even before, with the eagles of Napoleon, it penetrated the Pyrenees and lighted on the Escurial. And at this hour the mind of the Peninsula seethes in its deeps, with fanatic and abject superstition in fermenting combination with a wrathful, and libertine infidelity.

As, therefore, we inquire, how and with what consequence spiritual despotism has kept her arrogated charge of the world's faith, we are summoned by the muse of history to follow her at the close of the eighteenth century to the heights of the Alps and the Pyrenees, and look out on three historic landscapes—

realms of that despotism and the fairest climes of Europe. Standing there we look northward, and lo, a nation burns! monarchy, church, society, sink in the mighty conflagration. The fires of ruin are on throne, tower and temple. We seem to be looking at the opening of the sixth seal of the Revelation. The central scene is a vast mad-house where all the maniacs have broken their chains, burst their cells, and are burning their prisons; and the furies of the crimes of a thousand years, from many a red field of fight and massacre—from Bastiles and holy offices and sunless cells gloomy with midnight murder—hover over the revel of madness and death, scattering phrenzy and flame. "Lo!" says the muse of history, "one achievement of spiritual despotism." Faith she slew; but Atheism and Anarchy arose from its blood, avengers! Lo their Saturnalia! They drag herself to the funeral-pyre of her slain, and burn her in the conflagration she has prepared.

We look southward to the Spanish Peninsula, and lo! a land of silence and darkness and the shadow of death; "where the light is as darkness!" The dead are there. A ghostly terror, like that seen of Satan at the gates of Hell, sits alone in the gloom. Life, intellect, manhood, strength, honor, together with faith, lie in those living tombs at her feet, over which she keeps ward for ages; brandishing the terrors of the earthly sword and the pangs of eternal fire. "Lo," says the historic muse, "Lo, spiritual despotism keeping out infidelity from Spain! *Her victims in their deep sleep have no fever. There is no delirium in the grave.*"

We turn to that other land—the land of ancient story—clime of glory and of strength. We hear only a deep respiration as from the dungeon of ages! a mighty sigh as from a great people in mortal agony! We look, and lo, a nation faint and prostrate! with diadem and sceptre and broken sword and lyre in the dust beside her; the memories of empire and genius on her pale and haughty brow! Lo, there she lies, together with her glorious children —art, eloquence, philosophy and song, as well as faith, gasping under the ever-tightening folds of spiritual despotism—a Laocoon in the grasp of the Python! "Lo" again says the historic muse—"*Lo spiritual despotism protecting Italy from infidelity.*"

CONCLUSION.

RÉSUMÉ OF THE ARGUMENT.

Thus have we discussed as we have been able, in the course of our brief survey, our proposed theme, THE INFIDELITY OF THE EIGHTEENTH CENTURY. We have endeavored to describe and trace to its causes, that portentous eclipse of the faith of the world; have considered its relations to the religious wars of the previous historic period, the dethronement of the religious idea and the rise of Mammonism to the ascendency in European civilization; its relations to the revolution in philosophy, and the emancipation of mind in the sixteenth and seventeenth centuries, and to the despotisms, political and ecclesiastical, over Europe during the same period; and finally, to the peculiar position of France in European civilization and the elements in her constitution and history, generative and diffusive of infidelity. The great cause—the cause of causes—of the fearful phenomenon we are analyzing, we have found to be *not liberty in any form, but* SPIRITUAL DESPOTISM; wielded by monarchy or hierarchy and commonly by both, holding up a Church, made by this despotism imbecile, corrupt and tyrannical, between the world and Jesus Christ, and thus darkening the faith of nations.

In closing our review of this theme we wish to call attention to one most solemn aspect of it. In attempting to trace the great defection of Christendom from the Christian faith during the last two centuries, we think we find, as was indicated in a former chapter, their *causes to be rather practical than speculative, more moral than intellectual, less theological than ecclesiastic. The religious insurrection of nations was political and social, rather than metaphysical.* Their revolt was *less from Christianity than the Church;* or at least was from Christianity *because of the Church.* It was less a quarrel with dogma than with life, or it was with dogma because of life. So it was then: so it is now, and so it will be to the end. The world will read the living epistles of Christianity, more than even the written word. And its faith will be determined by the exhibition Christianity may make of itself in the life of individuals, communions and communities, more than in the schools of philosophy, or the halls of theologic debate. And we venture to predict that if the faith of the world ever suffers again a similar disaster, *it will be from similar causes;* it will be not on pantheism, materialism, fatalism, pelagianism, but on some great MORAL APOSTASY OR PRACTICAL WRONG, that primarily at least, it will be shipwrecked. Christianity then seemed to have allied itself with atrocious wrongs in society, to have become the champion of old and intolerable abuses and absurdities. And as men could not but distrust a religion which seemed to be in conflict with their conscience and moral sense, so they were compelled to hate one which threw itself across the path of human progress, opposed itself to social ameliorations and conspired with the oppressors and liberticides of the world.

Not the least fearful now, amid the signs of the times, are the present *social* aspect and aim of infidelity. Its dream and passion in both this country and Europe is not more a *theologic* than a *social* revolution. It rejects Christianity less because of the dogmas of the trinity, atonement, predestination, *than its championship or indulgence of political or social wrongs.* The human heart indeed may hate a religion that curbs its lusts. But until it *can mask that hatred behind some palpable wrong or absurdity*, it will be little likely to make much show of its hate; much less make it the nucleus of any extensive infidel combination or conspiracy. If we would utterly discomfit infidelity, we must take from it such masks. Christianity must be the great leader and guardian of reform, the religion of melioration, emancipation, and progress. Ceasing to be this, she draws on herself the incredulity and wrath of nations. Condemned by the moral judgment of mankind which she has herself instructed, she will be rejected of them; and society moving forward on a course of godless reform, will find itself embarked on an endless cycle of bootless revolution, convulsion and ruin.

The chief malign influence, which has thrown the spiritual power in society on a wrong course and placed it in a wrong position, as we have oft repeated and cannot urge too earnestly, has been that of spiritual despotism. True, we see infidelity spring upon society from many causes. But *she* is seen giving malignancy and, to a great extent, origin to all others.

Infidelity gushes upon Europe with the bloodshed of one hundred and fifty years of religious wars. But who opened that terrible wound in Christendom? Spiritual despotism. Infidelity arose upon Europe from the great philosophic revolution of modern history. But what made a revolution in itself so beneficent and essential to the progress of society, so disastrous in its consequences to religious faith? Spiritual despotism. Infidelity again, with the rise and ascendency of the idea of wealth, diffused itself through European civilization. But what made the ascendency of that idea so fatal to religious belief? And what made the golden stream, that poured on European society, with consequences so happy and so brilliant to other interests, so deadly to this? Spiritual despotism. The same evil cause we find also affecting disastrously the intellect, morals and manners of the spiritual order, and of the subject nations. Also, by presenting Christianity with a false aspect as a religion of force and cruelty, and fraud, and placing it in a false position as an ally of political despotism, and social wrongs, it draws on her the incredulity and rage of the oppressed millions. We have found her also, by investing the Church with the Nessian purple of her infallibility, converting it to an eternal conservator of all the lies, follies, mummeries, superstitions and crimes of the past; and obliging it to pass with all these before the derision of the ages, an apostle of unbelief to all the future.

Thus as between despotism and liberty, as was first started in this discussion, the question of comparative guilt in the great apostasy of the European mind from the Christian faith, admits but of one and that an obvious solution. That solution we think one of grave import to the two great philosophic and ecclesiastic schools, that are contending for the possession of modern society, and the modern

Church; which schools find their embodiment and representation in Romanism and Protestanism, in the essentially distinctive imports of these terms. Romanism is the incarnation or organization of the principle of spiritual despotism. This is the central organic principle, to which all its environment of rites, forms and orders, is but accident or incident. Of Protestanism on the other hand, in its ultimate essence, the life principle is spiritual liberty. All violations of this principle calling themselves by its name, are abuses and misnomers. Between Protestantism and Romanism, as properly representing their distinctive essential principles and different philosophic schools, the question of comparative blame for the "eclipse of faith" in the last century, admit of no hesitancy; between them as representing different *historic parties* the question becomes greatly changed. Still our answer though not as absolute, must be the same. The guilt of that shipwreck of the faith of the world, must be laid at the doors of that Church, that is the great embodiment of spiritual despotism on earth, and claims to be spiritual sovereign of mankind. To this grave charge she must plead at the bar of History and of God. Nor may any disposition to merge essential antagonisms and veil crimes of the past, in an era of universal good feeling, avail to silence this fearful arraignment, or screen her from the just indignation of the human race. While toward the men that are in her communion we would deal in all kindness and all charity, and would yield to none in love and admiration of the pure and noble names connected with it, the justice of history, the majesty and sanctity of truth, and principles that partake of the eternity and awfulness of God, will not allow us to forget that the *organic and central principle of that Church* is one of the deadliest and most malignant plagues that ever broke from the infernal pit to curse our world. with that principle the world can have no peace till it has driven it back to its own dark den again. The earth will be rent and torn till it is cast out. With any system, any Church, enshrining that principle, civilization and Christianity must wage perpetual war. Such a Church, though it wear the awe of vast ages; though the cloud of one thousand years veil its mysterious dome; though saintly faces without number look on you from painted window and pictured ceiling, and stories of heroic and martyr piety are lettered and figured all over the marble column and frescoed wall; and music like rift of angelic anthem, breathes through its "long-drawn aisles and fretted vaults;" yea, though the names of David, and Job, and Isaiah were there, nothing can save it. Against it all the human race will fight, against it all the true Church on earth; against it all the angels of God. The temple of all the muses, and the graces, and the virtues—let spiritual despotism once enter as tutelar genius, it becomes ultimately a cage of all doleful creatures. That spirit, wherever found, we believe to be essentially and immortally malignant, hateful to man and God; forbidding with itself all truce and all compromise; rending and tearing the earth till it is cast out. And into whatsoever ecclesiastic body it shall enter to possess it, we believe that body is destined to be hated of God and of all good and wise men, and that the saints shall war upon it and slay it, and burn it with fire.

As we close the discussion of our theme, we feel that the entire scope of the argument we have traversed, the general principles and inductions derived from it, and the scenes and facts of history adduced, all turn the eye in one direction in awe and fear. Toward one power calling itself of God, "sitting in the seat of God," the mind looks in fear of the things which both revelation and the philosophy of history announce as about to come upon her. Long since from bloody and woeful ages went up against her a cloud of accusation to the throne of God, crying out, "How long, O Lord, holy and true, dost thou not avenge our blood on them that dwell on the earth?"

But now we hear another voice added to those under the altar—a cry from the darkened million in the deeps below her stupendous cathedrals—a blinded Agonistes groping in agony of revenge and despair "for the pillars," and exclaiming, "Strengthen me, I pray Thee, this once, O God, that I may be avenged for my two eyes." Indeed that power must stand arraigned at the bar of history, of the crime of almost quenching the spiritual vision of a century, and that century one of the most powerful and brilliant in human annals. When we look at these thickening accusations of history against that power, giving up so many ages, and believe a God of history, though long He hideth Himself, still dwelleth on high, terror takes hold of us. Already there seems to us a fearful convergency of signs in the aspect of the times, and in the Book of God, looking toward her; that a day tempestuous with the long-stayed anger of God and the indignation of the human race, hastens. And when it burns on her proud structures, amid all her names of blasphemy that shall be made to kindle and to stand out upon her in letters of fire to the scorn and hate of Earth and Heaven, not least amid title of arraignment and sentence on her brow, shall flame out, MOTHER OF INFIDELITY.

THE END.

www.ingramcontent.com/pod-product-compliance
Lightning Source LLC
LaVergne TN
LVHW010239110826
845151LV00004B/1338

* 9 7 8 1 4 2 5 5 2 4 4 6 3 *